On Sundays

Long lunches through the seasons

Hardie Grant

BOOKS

Dave Verheul

with Royce Akers

Contents

Foreword
Tony Tan

I can still remember my first encounter with chef Dave Verheul's food. It all began in 2013. Some friends from hospitality mentioned a wine bar called The Town Mouse in Carlton, an inner-city suburb in Melbourne's bohemian quarter. They raved about the food and the natural wine list. I was intrigued by the name and immediately wanted to check it out. So, on one cold autumnal evening, I ventured into this tiny bolthole in Drummond Street.

I was expecting a pleasant evening filled with merriment aided by the excellent wine list curated by co-owner Christian McCabe, but I didn't expect that this evening would become the beginning of my love affair with Dave's cooking.

I still recall the sensation of biting into what looked to be an ordinary profiterole and how it shattered my perception of what choux pastry could be. Dave's version was a work of wonder: the choux was filled with parmesan and black pepper, it was baked and then finished off in a dehydrator to give it extra crunch. Then it was filled with the silkiest goat's cheese mousse, sprinkled with caraway and thyme before it arrived sitting on honey collected from the roof top. Talk about layer upon layer of flavours: salty, sweet, earthy and crunchy. In short, it was a triumph of epic proportions.

I can also remember his oysters opened to order. They arrived plump and pert served alongside a sorbet made with chardonnay vinegar. I thought it was a brilliant combination because the delicate vinegar sorbet with its softer flavour worked perfectly with the creaminess of the oysters. At that time, I thought this guy certainly knew how to combine flavour combinations, but little did I know that Dave cannot eat oysters, which goes to prove that he's a master of his craft.

I walked away that evening filled with awe and curiosity about this chef. Who is he? Where did he come from? And why is his food so much fun to eat and that it gives me goosebumps? It's the kind of food that just says 'eat me!'

Like most chefs, this soft-spoken legend has cut his chef's teeth in some snazzy restaurants in Australia, England and his native New Zealand. But while experience and technique are important, it is Dave's unique ability to hone in his creations that make his cooking so special. Dave's quiet energy and the way he speaks about his approach to food and cooking set him apart. His food looks fresh and effortless, but this is built upon years and years of dedication. And obsession.

ON SUNDAYS

Which brings me to this cookbook. Dave is a wonderful human being who cares deeply about sustainability, seasonality, generosity and the world we live in, and this book reflects all of these elements. Just like at his restaurants, this food is peppered with clarity and flavour. In other words, I love the concise explanation that sits with each recipe – and I can almost taste some of the dishes featured here because they evoke the many happy moments I've had eating Dave's food. I also love snippets of wisdom about preserving and cannot forget the humour scattered through the book. I love the whimsy of vin John.

Fast forward to 2015 and I find Dave in downtown Melbourne at Embla. A wine bar slash restaurant co-owned by Christian McCabe and Dave, it was an instant success due to its excellent service, great wine list, fabulous food and a lively atmosphere. By now Dave's reputation as one of the best chefs in the country is well and truly recognised, not only by the public but also by his peers. But he is not one to rest on his laurels and the dishes he dispenses from the wood-fired oven and grill are as thrilling they have ever been.

His soured cucumber with creamed feta and dusted dill powder is so bloody delicious that I cannot resist ordering it every time I'm there. As for his roast chicken, seared skin side down and finished off in the wood-fired oven and presented with an impeccable jus with a subtle whisper of smokiness that is sigh inducing. It's etched in my memory forever.

And that bread! If ever bread is taken to define a restaurant's commitment to excellence or that of a chef's, Dave's bread sums up what he's all about. Great sourdough bread requires painstaking care, knowledge of techniques and a lot of patience, passion and intuition. More than anything, it has to have soul. Every time I eat his bread, be it served with kombu butter or with shiitake oil and macadamia cream, it is crusty, flavourful and dare I say voluptuous.

God! The foreword is turning into a love fest. Well, it is. From the moment I had my first bite of Dave's insanely delicious profiterole and his bread, I was hooked. I think it has a lot to do with his recognition of talent and mutual respect mixed with a healthy dose of humility. Anyone who has eaten Dave's food knows it's exciting, inspiring and sings with originality. His cookbook – this book – is all that.

– Tony Tan

ON SUNDAYS

Introduction

I quite like Sundays.
I'm guessing you do too.

For the first twenty or so years since starting in kitchens, it was rare to get one off. Even so, the pace and feeling of a Sunday service, as opposed to a kinetic Friday or Saturday night, made it one of the nicer shifts to work. The effortless connectedness of it. The relaxed mode the diners seemed, in most cases, to be in. And, in the kitchen, the sense of being nearly at the finish line. The opportunity, after one last push, to clean everything down and switch off for a couple of days. Like all good recipes, the sum of these parts would create a kind of immaculate vibe. On a really good Sunday, you'd be reminded of what you loved about cooking and, by extension, the restaurant business as a whole.

Exactly what that is can be hard to pin down. It probably changes as you go along. But at Embla, it does manifest as that same sort of sum-of-the-parts experience a good Sunday would offer up. In fact, when we started to put on set menu Sunday lunches, something about those services would feel very true to what Embla was built around: simple things grown by the best and cooked with care. Clear, vibrant flavours served with minimum distraction. But more than just the food, it was the tables full of people who chose to forego getting the lawns or laundry done in favour of connecting with loved ones over a shared meal. To this day, whenever we're hosting an event, we do our best to schedule it on a Sunday. It's just a more thoughtful and deliberate moment in time.

With all of that said, I have to admit I don't work many weekends anymore. Outside of the above-mentioned special events (or the occasional day spent bottling aperitifs) I'm once again doing weekends on the other side of the pass. This return to the general population has given me the chance to connect with so many people who for years existed in a separate time zone. Now, instead of being spent in the same kitchen with the same crew, Sundays are much less predictable – and that's great. But the thing they have in common, if you get them right, is the way they can heal you and set you up for the week to come. Getting it right means good food and good people.

Stands to reason that when it came time to compile a book of recipes created over my years at Embla, Town Mouse and beyond, the theme of Sundays was already on my mind. And the theme fits. Many of these aren't weekday meals you can make quickly after work. Not that this makes them better or worse. They're recipes that are fairly, for want of a better word, Sunday-ish. Tackling them, some more than others, will require a bit of headspace. They're also meals that have a bit of occasion about them. I don't always cook like this at home. Midweek, you'll find me tossing together a carbonara with the best of them. But when the right combination of time, motivation and people arises, this is the kind of food I enjoy dishing up.

The recipes in this book are divided into hypothetical Sunday lunches. Some might centre on a specific mood or moment in the year. Seasons are a particular focus, as I'm a big believer in making use of produce when it's at its peak. Others are designed around loosely outlined social scenarios – things to pick at while sitting by a warm fire on a weekend in the country, for example. In these pages you'll find menus to cook at the height of citrus season, or things to prepare when you or a friend have had a tough week. There are full-blown open-pit barbecues you can throw to mark the welcome return of good weather, as well as intimate, intricate dishes to make for loved ones it's been too long since you've last seen.

Growing up in New Zealand, Sundays were always about mum's classic lamb roast. Even after I'd gotten older and moved to another town, I always tried to be front and centre when she brought it out of the oven. No matter what mischief you'd put yourself through that week, that meal – and the conversations you had around it – made you whole again. And while these recipes may be a little more involved than my mum's roast, this book is about that same feeling, and being able to share it with the people you love. I hope you enjoy it.

'Like all good recipes, the sum
of these parts would create a
kind of immaculate vibe.'

How to use this book

Almost all of these recipes use either a wood-fired oven, a fire built on wood, or both. If this isn't possible at home, then I can suggest that you use either a good quality gas-fired pizza oven or turn your oven up as hot as that guy can go. As for replicating a wood-fired grill at home, you could use a hot gas grill (broiler), but it won't be quite the same. We use both of these cooking mediums in the restaurant as they're a fun, direct and incredibly tactile way to cook. It requires you to stay closely engaged in the process and that can only make you a better cook. I am by no means your mother, but cooking over fire can hurt. It's potentially incredibly dangerous so please be careful.

The recipes here are the exact same ones we've used at Embla over the years. They're meant to be tweaked and adjusted with the seasons, so use them as a guide. Make your own mark on them. Change the vinegar, swap the vegetable – whatever you want.

Most ingredients in this book are listed by weight, and I like it like that. Measuring jugs are always wrong and can really throw a pastry recipe out. If you weigh everything then you only ever need one measuring tool, and it's fast as hell.

A lot of these recipes require a fair amount of foresight so give them a read through before you begin to cook.

We work year round to build up a pantry of preserves to use throughout the year. An ingredient preserved at its peak of flavour could wind up being the exact element a dish is missing months down the road, or provide an enlivening glimpse of summertime in the middle of winter. Asian grocery stores are a goldmine for delicious things like preserved yuzu and shio koji liquid. If you have issues sourcing any of these items, feel free to sub in something similar.

You'll probably notice we use Fermented fennel juice (see page 225) in just about everything. It's an incredible flavour booster for any vegetarian recipe and it tends to brighten anything you use it in.

Some other things I love and use a lot of: fennel, all kinds of nuts, sunflower seeds, fennel, fermented tomato juice, fennel, garlic, all citrus, fennel.

These menus are by no means meant to be prescriptive. Mix them up and cook them any way you want. I just want you to cook them and have fun with it.

13

Buying produce

Like a lot of chefs these days, I've always tried to work directly with small local organic or biodynamic vegetable farms, and at Embla it's no different. Choosing to work this way has a number of benefits. The first is that all of the money goes directly to the farmers who are actually growing our produce. Secondly, these farmers really bloody care about the things they grow. This love and attention shines through in the produce. Thirdly, these passionate farmers often grow vegetables that have fallen off the radars of commercial bulk vegetable growers.

The vegetable world is large and diverse but you wouldn't know it. We're finding ourselves more and more funnelled into using the same old veggies over and over. Just take a look at what's on offer at your local supermarkets and you'll see what I mean. Heirloom vegetables, for example, are thought to be too tricky to grow, too hard to pick and transport, or just too much of a risk to take up shelf space. It's a damn shame and it's also really boring. Thank god for small growers, and the same can be said for all our producers.

You might be thinking that establishing relationships with incredible small-scale producers is something reserved for restaurant people, but it's not. In the home context the best way to buy your produce is from your local farmer's market. I do realise that this requires a lot more effort. But while you won't be able to get everything you need in one place, you will buy produce that has been grown responsibly, sustainably and, presumably, without nasty sprays and insecticides. You will directly support someone's family and connect with the passionate hard-working people who choose to grow our food.

You'll also see the seasons come and go, and taste first-hand how this affects the produce. Produce is seasonal for a reason. Try eating a fresh peach in the middle of winter. It just doesn't feel right. Hearty vegetables grow when your body needs them. The same goes for vibrant leafy greens, which come along when your body craves freshness in the spring. I know it sounds like hippie bumper sticker talk, but it's true: we're connected with the things we eat in more ways than one.

Get amongst it. Touch and taste and smell. Ask whoever's selling about how they grow, how they raise the cattle, or how they get the milk for the cheese. If they're passionate – as most producers are – they'll be more than happy to tell you. In no time you'll not only have your own set of expert suppliers, you and your loved ones will be eating a lot better for it.

Equipment

(1)

ON SUNDAYS

(1) Wood grill

Our grill at Embla sits right alongside the wood oven and often they're worked as almost a single entity. Wood and coals are juggled from one to the other whenever one needs more or less. We burn an Australian hardwood called red gum on the grill, for the reasons described below, but also because of its flavour. We cook both fast and slow over fire as you will see in the following chapters, so the flavour of the smoke here is important.

When grilling over fire, the key steps are lighting your fire early, building it up until it is burning decent-sized logs, and then letting it burn down enough so that you've formed a bed of embers and the flame is no longer a raging yellow – raging flames will make your food taste like petrol. Once you have a bed of embers, add new logs on one side of the fire and cook on the other, keeping the embers fed with new fuel.

(2) Wood oven

This is the big one. At the heart of Embla is a hulking great wood-fired oven, and probably 90 per cent of the menu is touched by either the wood oven or the fire it produces. We do have other ovens, both convection and steam ones, but these are solely used for certain prep jobs. The flavour you get from cooking with a wood oven is like nothing else, and – in my opinion – this shines brightest when cooking vegetables.

Throughout this book, I'll talk (possibly too much) about the direct force and delicacy you can achieve when cooking with an oven like this. It's a primal, base-level way of cooking that requires you to use your senses and stay engaged. And to throw you another opinion, I think it makes you a better cook.

Wood ovens can take a long time to get up to heat, mostly because the stone floor in most ovens is very thick. Once you get it up to temperature the beauty of this is that the heat rising off this stone gives you a second heat source on top of the actual fire itself, which is how bakers use wood ovens without a direct coal bed. This is where the delicacy part comes in – you can cook at an extreme temperature without your food becoming scorched or dehydrated. To give you an idea of what I mean, a boned-out roast chicken in our 500°C (932°F) oven cooks in about 8 minutes and always comes out perfectly juicy and tender.

For firing our oven, we use an Australian hardwood called red gum. For what we do and how we use it, red gum strikes a good balance between cost and burn time, which is important in a commercial sense when you go through over a tonne of it every week. As for giving off a bunch of smoke, a wood oven will only produce smoke up to about 250°C (482°F), at which point it should burn fairly clean, which is good for the environment and the washing on your neighbour's clothesline.

(2)

(3) Grill sieves

We use all manner of sieves for grilling over fire in the restaurant. They are great for handling things like clams or loose vegetables as it would be painful turning each individual item on a rack. We especially like the wide tamis-style sieve; these have a large flat area which makes it easy to cook larger volumes evenly. I recommend seasoning a new sieve over a low flame for 5–10 minutes.

(4) Grill cages

Grill cages are a very handy tool for grilling over fire. They make manoeuvring and adjusting to your fire extremely quick and easy. They're especially handy when cooking fish over a fire. Often the fish skin will stick to your grill rack until it begins to brown, and the cages ensure you can control the heat up until that point.

(5) Cast-iron pans

I mean, what isn't better when cooked in a cast-iron pan? Cast iron really shines over fire. Often the heat extremes involved in cooking with fire mean things can scorch easily, and using cast iron acts as a buffer. It does take a little getting used to. It's slower to heat and retains heat for much longer than a home-style pan, and you need to keep this in mind when cooking delicate items.

For the majority of things cooked in this book you will need three types of pans:

- Low-sided, cast-iron skillet – great for when you want the full blast of the fire to hit the sides of the item being cooked.

- 50 mm (2 in) deep cast-iron frying pan, preferably around 25 cm (10 in) in diameter. This is your everyday go-to wood oven pan, great for roasting a chicken or cooking down escarole for a pasta dish.

- Deep, large cast-iron pot with a lid. This is perfect for braising vegetables, baking your bread or anything that is wet.

The beauty of cast iron is that if you take care of it, it should last you many good years. So it's worth spending money on a decent brand.

(6) Meat mallet

You don't often see meat mallets around these days but they're an excellent tool for bashing out everything from veal scallopini to the tuna carpaccio dish in this book (see page 155). They're also a great tension release.

(7) Terracotta cookware

Terracotta has been used for centuries to cook over fire, and who are we to break that tradition? Make sure you soak your terracotta in cold water for at least 8 hours before using to ensure that it doesn't crack while being heated.

(8) Bread bannetons

We use cane bread bannetons in the restaurant for all of our sourdough. As the bread dough has a fairly high hydration percentage, bannetons provide much needed support while resting through the bulk ferment stage. You can find them at chef supply stores or online. Make sure to dry and scrape clean between uses to prevent any mould from growing.

(9) Dough scraper

A very handy and cheap tool for shaping bread.

(10) Cake-testing pin

The best $4 you'll ever spend. Chefs use them to check the internal temperature of everything. Simply insert the pin into the densest part of what you're cooking, leave to warm for 10 seconds then remove and hold against the inside of your wrist. Not an exact science, but still extremely effective.

(11) Vacuum sealer

Home versions of these vacuum-packing machines are super handy. They're great for prepping food to freeze and are an essential tool for fermenting small amounts of produce.

(12) Dehydrator

We use commercial-grade dehydrators in the restaurant as they are able to operate at lower temperatures. The low temperatures, combined with an uneven pulsing airflow, help to preserve peak flavour with a faster drying time. This is especially important when you are drying delicate things like herbs. Having said this, even domestic dehydrators can be used a bunch of different ways to open up new flavour and texture opportunities.

(5)

(8)

(9)

Ingredients

Cream

It sounds like a strange statement but it can be difficult to find good cream. Often what you find in stores has been thickened with either gelatine or another hydrocolloid. All cream used in the following recipes is 38 per cent fat, which is sometimes, but not reliably, labelled as 'pure cream'. If you're having trouble finding it, try buying yours from a good local dairy producer – chances are they haven't messed with theirs!

Eggs

Recipes in this book use large eggs, however size, weight and labelling can very across countries and brands. Where a precise measurement is called for, in pastry recipes for example, a weight of egg yolks or whites has been provided.

Milk

All milk called for in this book is full-cream (whole) milk unless stated otherwise.

Olive oil

We use an extra-virgin arbequina olive oil from an incredible local producer, Mount Zero, for all of our olive oil. It has punch and it has personality. We use this oil for its incredible flavour and don't tend to cook with it too often. Most lower-grade olive oils are heat or chemically extracted and, to be honest, there are better, healthier oils to cook with.

Salt

We use fine table salt for all seasoning in the restaurant and good quality table salt for any bulk seasoning needs.

Sugar

We use a fine caster (superfine) sugar as our go-to pastry sugar unless stated otherwise.

A Sunday at the
beginning of spring

Spring has different meanings in different places. Around Australia there are plenty of places that barely even have a winter. Then there's Melbourne, which can be so miserable through July and August that it could almost be London. Well, not quite.

But if there's one consistent thing to celebrate at this time of year, it's the spring produce coming back into season. Those flavours, colours and textures you didn't realise you were missing until you get a glimpse of them at your local market. This menu is a celebration of that.

Serves 4

(1)   Fried globe artichoke, tarragon cream

(2)   Raw veal, peas, wild rocket, tonnato

(3)   Chickpea pancake, parsley, artichoke, Comté

(4)   Frozen ricotta, rhubarb, olive oil and rose geranium

ON SUNDAYS

Fried globe artichoke, tarragon cream

Artichokes are the budding flower of a certain type of thistle, so no wonder they can be a bastard to cook. Here we're using the globe variety, which is the least troublesome artichoke. You can boil them ahead to save time, something we'd definitely do in a restaurant kitchen. Kids of the eighties may recognise the tarragon cream: a play on green goddess sauce, a staple of *Women's Weekly* dinner party compendiums.

Artichokes
2 very large globe artichokes

Tarragon cream
30 g (1 oz) spinach
½ garlic clove, peeled
125 g (4½ oz) mayonnaise
80 g (2¾ oz) sour cream
5 g (⅛ oz) parsley, leaves only
20 g (¾ oz) tarragon, leaves only

To serve
vegetable oil, for frying
100 g (3½ oz) tapioca flour
20 g (¾ oz) dried oregano, ground

Artichokes

Find a pot large enough to hold both of the artichokes and fill it two-thirds of the way with cold water. Season the water well with salt. Using your hands, take the artichoke and start snapping off the tough outer leaves one by one until the leaves begin to turn a light green colour. The lighter in colour the leaf is, the more tender it is. Carefully trim the choke heart and cut where the stem meets the choke heart. Place the cleaned artichoke in the water and weigh down with a smaller pot to keep the artichokes submerged while they cook. Bring the water to a simmer over a medium heat and cook gently until tender. You can check this by inserting a cake-testing pin. Remove from the water and place, leaf side down, to drain and cool.

Tarragon cream

Bring a small pot of water to the boil and season well with salt. Quickly blanch the spinach and refresh in ice-cold water. Once it is cold, drain and squeeze any excess water out using your hands. Blend the spinach and remaining ingredients together in a small jug using a hand-held blender and season to taste with salt.

To serve

If you happen to have a deep-fryer at home turn that fella on and set the temperature to 170°C (340°F). If not, fill a responsibly sized pot halfway with vegetable oil. Gently heat to 170°C (340°F) while testing the temperature with a cooking thermometer.

Mix the tapioca flour and oregano together in a bowl. Take each artichoke and dredge it through the flour until completely covered, then tap firmly to remove any excess flour. You want to have a fairly light coating, so make sure that it hasn't clumped in any spots inside the leaves. Very carefully lower the artichokes, leaf side down, into the oil and fry until lightly golden, turning over midway through to help them cook evenly. Remove from the oil, season well with salt and leave to drain, leaf side down, on some paper towel. Once cool enough to handle transfer onto two serving plates and spoon the tarragon cream into the centre of each artichoke. This will help to cool the heart somewhat. Eat by picking off the leaves one by one and dipping the lower, tender part into the cream.

Raw veal, peas, wild rocket, tonnato

We're riffing here on a classic vitello tonnato and our goal is freshness. Tender raw cubes of veal replace the traditional poached slices. The pop of just-podded peas breaks up the meaty texture. Shio delivers a turbocharged citrus umami note. Wild rocket busts it all up with its peppery bigness.

Veal
150 g (5½ oz) veal rump

Shio dressing
60 g (2 oz) lemon or
  plain shio koji (page 225)
30 g (1 oz) lemon juice
30 g (1 oz) olive oil

Tonnato cream
150 g (5½ oz) olive oil
50 g (1¾ oz) tuna
½ small rosemary sprig
2 g (¹⁄₁₆ oz) fresh oregano
1 garlic clove, peeled
25 g (1 oz) olive brine
25 g (1 oz) vegetable oil
lemon juice, to taste

To serve
¼ shallot, very finely diced
50 g (1¾ oz) fresh peas, podded
10 g (¼ oz) wild rocket (arugula)

Shio dressing

You can either make your own lemon shio koji (see page 225), or most good Japanese grocery stores will have shio koji liquid. Mix all the ingredients together until emulsified using a whisk or a hand-held blender. Season to taste with a little salt if needed.

Tonnato cream

To cook the tuna, take a small pot and add 100 g (3½ oz) of the olive oil, the tuna, rosemary, oregano and garlic. Season with a little salt and place the pot over a very low heat to warm. You want to cook the tuna very gently here; it should take around 30 minutes and the temperature should never get above 55°C (130°F). Once the tuna is cooked through and the fish flakes easily, remove the fish and chill quickly.

Place the chilled tuna and brine into a small high-sided jug and blend with a hand-held blender until smooth-ish. Combine the vegetable oil with the remaining olive oil and slowly add to the tuna mix until emulsified and smooth. Season with sea salt and lemon juice to taste.

To serve

Place the veal into a small mixing bowl, season with a little salt and black pepper. Add a little diced shallot and the peas, and dress with a little of the shio dressing. Mix to combine. Lightly tear the rocket into manageable-sized pieces and add to the bowl. Scoop a couple of spoons of the tonnato cream onto two serving dishes, give the veal mix a final toss and place on top of the cream on both plates.

Chickpea pancake, parsley, artichoke, Comté

The key with these pancakes is getting a perfect crusty edge, so you're going to want a lot of heat. The wood-fired oven at Embla burns upwards of 500°C (932°F) and you can achieve that pretty easily in most home pizza ovens (even those portable LPG ones). For those relying on a regular oven, we've included a few pointers on how to get to the required temp.

Pancake batter

50 g (1¾ oz) chickpea flour (besan)

Charred parsley salsa verde

100 g (3½ oz) parsley, leaves only
10 g (¼ oz) vegetable oil
50 g (1¾ oz) basil leaves
25 g (1 oz) capers
½ shallot, peeled
½ garlic clove, peeled
50 g (1¾ oz) olive oil

To finish

40 g (1½ oz) vegetable oil
¼ small rosemary sprig, chopped
3–4 baby globe artichokes, cleaned
    (see page 27) and submerged
    in lemon water
½ small shallot, finely diced
50 g (1¾ oz) parsley, leaves only
Lemon dressing (page 225), to serve
60 g (2 oz) 12-month-old Comté

Pancake batter

Place the chickpea flour, 150 g (5½ oz) water and a good pinch of salt into a small container. Whisk everything together and leave to hydrate in the fridge for a minimum of 3 hours.

Charred parsley salsa verde

Place the parsley into a small bowl, dress with the veg' oil, season lightly with sea salt and give a solid mix to coat the leaves. By coating the leaves in oil, you will ensure the herbs grill instead of turning into something that tastes like petrol. Transfer the leaves to a grilling sieve and grill over a high heat until one-third of the leaves are dark. Make sure you give them a mix while grilling so that they cook evenly. Add the grilled parsley leaves to a hand-held blender with the rest of the ingredients and blitz until you have a coarse but homogenous consistency. Season to taste with salt and set aside.

To finish

Classically, chickpea pancakes, or farinata, are always cooked in a wood oven as the oven gets hot enough to finish the job quickly, meaning the outer edges are crispy while the inside stays soft. The flavour it imparts is also a huge drawcard. Unless you have the luxury of a wood oven at home you are going to need to recreate the pure intensity in your home oven or a gas-fired pizza oven. Preheat your wood or gas pizza oven to 450°C (842°F). If using a convection oven, you will have to turn it up as high as possible, use the fan-forced setting and, if your oven allows, turn the grill (broiler) on too!

Take a large cast-iron pan and warm it on your stovetop. Add the oil and swirl to coat the wall of the pan. Give the chickpea batter one last mix and add half of the batter to the pan along with a little of the chopped rosemary and a healthy pinch of salt. Place into your raging electric wood oven and cook for around 6 minutes. It should be caramelised around the edges and nicely brown on both the top and bottom. You want to create texture during the cook as the middle will always stay soft. Once cooked, transfer to a serving plate. Repeat with the remaining mixture.

Take the baby artichokes and, using a mandolin, slice as finely as you can. Put the artichokes into a small bowl, dress with some of the lemon dressing and season well with salt and black pepper. Add the diced shallot and parsley and mix lightly. Take the parsley salsa verde and spoon over the top of the pancakes. Top this with the artichoke and parsley mix and then finely grate the Comté over the top.

Frozen ricotta, rhubarb, olive oil and rose geranium

The standard dessert at our house growing up was ice cream with fruit. I'm still a fan. One thing to note: on its way to becoming ice cream, the milk here is first made into ricotta. This may seem like an extra step for no reason, but the texture of the result is silky and worth the effort.

Ricotta
900 g (2 lb) milk
150 g (5½ oz) cream
3 g (⅒ oz) coriander seeds
1 g (1/32 oz) rosemary leaves
3 g (⅒ oz) citric acid

Frozen ricotta
275 g (9½ oz) ricotta (see above)
200 g (7 oz) cream
150 g (5½ oz) egg whites
130 g (4½ oz) sugar

Olive oil meringue
75 g (2¾ oz) egg whites
120 g (4½ oz) sugar
30 g (1 oz) strongly-flavoured olive oil

Ricotta

Put the milk and cream in a small pot. Wrap the coriander seeds and rosemary in a little square of muslin (cheesecloth), tie it tight, then add it to the dairy mix. Warm over a low–medium heat until it reaches 90°C (194°F). The trick here is to not stir it too much – as I believe it affects the texture – but enough that it doesn't scorch on the bottom of the pan. When it comes to temperature, tip in the citric acid and gently stir once to disperse it evenly. Take off the heat and leave it undisturbed for 15 minutes. Use a slotted spoon to scoop off the ricotta curds and drain. Keep the whey for making the Frozen ricotta, below.

Frozen ricotta

Make a ricotta puree by using some of the whey produced when making your ricotta (see above). Blend a portion of the fresh ricotta with enough whey to create a thick but fluid consistency, similar to medium whipped cream. In a bowl, use a whisk to whip the cream to soft peaks. Put the egg whites in the bowl of a stand mixer fitted with the whisk attachment. Turn to medium–high speed and add the sugar slowly to make a simple meringue. The idea is that you want to begin adding the sugar earlier than traditional meringues so that you end up with something that is denser, as this will help the final frozen texture. Using a flat spatula, carefully fold the whipped cream into the ricotta mix then, finally, the meringue into the cream mix. Pour the mixture into a container so that it comes around 3 cm (1¼ in) up the side of the container. Freeze for at least 4 hours. When completely frozen take a 9 cm (3½ in) pastry ring cutter and punch out four discs. You can snack on the trim or keep frozen for another time.

Olive oil meringue

Put the whites into the bowl of a stand mixer fitted with a whisk attachment and add a small pinch of salt. Put the sugar and 60 g (2 oz) water in a small pan and cook over a medium heat until it reaches 117°C (243°F) on a sugar thermometer. Turn the mixer up to high speed and slowly add the sugar syrup. Continue mixing until the meringue cools, then add the olive oil. Transfer the meringue to a piping (pastry) bag and chill in the fridge. This recipe will make slightly too much, but it is difficult to whip in any smaller quantity.

Rhubarb

250 g (9 oz) blood plums
150 g (5½ oz) sweet white wine
100 g (3½ oz) sugar
15 g (½ oz) rose geranium leaves
3 thin rhubarb stems

Rhubarb

Take the blood plums and, using a small knife, cut them in half, remove the pits and then place into a small blender. Pulse until the flesh has broken up. Press this pulp through a fine-mesh sieve to obtain around 200 g (7 oz) of juice. Bring the wine, sugar and 150 g (5½ oz) water to the boil in a small saucepan. Add the rose geranium leaves, remove from the heat, cover and leave to infuse for an hour. Once cooled, remove the leaves and add the plum juice. Working one stem at a time, slice the rhubarb with a sharp knife on as steep an angle and as thinly as possible. Ideally you want a slice that is around 4 cm (1½ in) long. Put all of the sliced rhubarb into the pan with the rose geranium syrup and warm very gently, to around body temperature. Immediately transfer to a container and chill.

To finish

Place the frozen ricotta in the bottom of a serving bowl. Pipe the meringue around the top outer edge of the ricotta. Drain the rhubarb slices and carefully place in a spiral pattern on top of the ricotta and meringue, finish with a little of the remaining syrup.

A Sunday lunch,
long overdue

What we love about Sunday lunches – that they are, in a way, sacred, but also laid back, low pressure and inherently special – makes them perfect for those mini reunions that keep sliding down the calendar.

The idea here is an overdue Sunday lunch that's full of little connection points. Dishes that you tear into and share. A tender hunk of meat hanging over a fire pit, perfect for chatting around. Nothing too finicky that will take you out of the conversation for too long. After all, if you wanted to be stuck in a kitchen while others have all the fun, you'd be a chef.

Serves 4

(1) Burrata, spring vegetables, walnut and green chilli

(2) Pork rack cooked over the fire

(3) Asparagus, buttermilk, frisée, grapefruit blossom

(4) Cherries, shiso, yuzu and salted coconut ice cream

ON SUNDAYS

Burrata, spring vegetables, walnut and green chilli

More and more of us are growing our own beautiful veggies at home. The next level up is pickling. Lock in those gains. Preserve all of that hard-earned produce. Here we have a simple and adaptable pickling base – feel free to experiment. Here, the sharp crunch of your veggies is played off against the creaminess of fresh burrata, with a little green chilli heat.

Pickled vegetables

350 g (12½ oz) white vinegar

150 g (5½ oz) champagne vinegar

100 g (3½ oz) sugar

30 g (1 oz) salt

1 onion, sliced

1 bay leaf

1 tablespoon caraway seeds, lightly toasted

1 tablespoon coriander seeds, lightly toasted

1 tablespoon black peppercorns

2 garlic cloves, peeled

750 g (1 lb 11 oz) spring vegetables of your choice, e.g. golden beetroot (beets), purple-sprouting broccoli, white asparagus, young globe artichokes, broad beans, etc.

Fermented green chilli condiment

250 g (9 oz) Fermented green chilli (see page 225)

2 garlic cloves, peeled

50 g (1¾ oz) coriander (cilantro) leaves and stems

30 g (1 oz) parsley, leaves only

25 g (1 oz) sherry vinegar

¼ teaspoon ground black pepper

1 tablespoon cumin seeds, lightly toasted

50 g (1¾ oz) walnuts

100 g (3½ oz) olive oil

To finish

1 baby cucumber

2 purple radishes

olive oil

1 burrata

crostini or bread, to serve

Pickled vegetables

Put all ingredients, except the spring vegetables, into an appropriately sized pot with 900 g (2 lb) water and bring almost to the boil. Remove the pot from the heat and leave in a warm spot to infuse for an hour. Strain the pickle base into a clean pot. You can now use this pickling liquid to cook each vegetable individually. So, for instance, if you are cooking a beetroot, which is fairly dense in structure, then you will need to simmer it until it is tender, then cool. On the other end of the spectrum if you are pickling a snow pea (mangetout) then just pouring hot pickle liquid over it will be enough to cook it through. If you do find yourself with an excess of time on your hands, you could use the same pickle base but tailor the aromats in each to the specific vegetable you wish to cook in it – the world is your pickled oyster.

Fermented green chilli condiment

This sauce can definitely be made if you haven't fermented some green chillies beforehand, just use a green chilli that isn't too hot. The fermented chillies will just add a bright, sour gooey-ness that makes it very complex. Put everything except the olive oil in a small bowl blender and blend until the herbs have broken down. Add the olive oil slowly then season to taste with salt. This will make way too much, but it is delicious on almost anything, particularly with eggs on toast in the morning, and it keeps for about a week in the fridge.

To finish

Remove a few pieces of each vegetable from its pickle and cut down into bite-sized shapes. Cut the cucumber and radishes into similar sized pieces. Put them all into a small bowl and add around 50 g (1¾ oz) of the pickling liquid, along with a good splash of olive oil and a healthy dose of salt and black pepper. Place a spoonful of the green chilli condiment on one side of your serving plate, arrange the vegetables around, pour over the dressing liquid and top with the burrata. Serve with crostini or bread on the side.

Pork rack cooked over the fire

You've got to love a dish where 95 per cent of the prep time consists of lighting your fire. That's the simple beauty of this type of cooking. A good cut of meat, a little salt and oil, and a well-maintained source of heat. The result is every bit as impressive as the process. People say fire stops being fascinating when you have to use it every day. I use it most days and I'm still fascinated.

4 points of a Berkshire
    pork rack, skin on
vegetable oil

You really want to cook this over a proper fire, so get it started 45 minutes before you would like to start cooking your pork. Establish a solid base of coals by letting each log burn down until there's minimal yellow flame. You are going to want to position the pork about 1 metre (3.2 feet) above the fire bed. Some home grills and fireplaces have inbuilt shelves, which are great, or you could suspend a rack above the grill – feel free to get creative here! For the best results, lightly score the skin and leave uncovered in your fridge overnight so that the skin dries as much as possible. Remove the rack from the fridge when you light the fire so that it comes to room temperature. Once you are ready to cook, lightly oil the whole rack and season well with sea salt. Place skin side down high over the fire and cook slowly for around an hour, move it around gently during this time so that the heat is evenly dispersed over the whole piece of meat. Once the skin has nicely blistered, flip the meat over, bone side down, and cook for another 15 minutes or so. Test using a cooking thermometer inserted into the thickest part of the meat. You want it to get to around 50°C (122°F) internally. Once it has reached temperature take it off the heat, cover loosely with aluminium foil and leave to rest for 5–10 minutes. When ready to serve carve in between the rib bones to make four separate cutlets.

ON SUNDAYS

Asparagus, buttermilk, frisée, grapefruit blossom

Apologies if this seems like I'm overthinking it, but asparagus is mostly about the white part in the centre. The fatter the spear, the crunchier that white bit stays. Get it while you can because, as the season goes on, you'll notice the asparagus at your grocer getting more and more slender (AKA sadder). Here it's paired with crème fraîche and a fragrant and simple to make blossom oil. You will need to start the grapefruit blossom oil a day ahead.

Buttermilk sauce

100 g (3½ oz) cultured buttermilk, chilled
20 g (¾ oz) Dijon mustard
30 g (1 oz) crème fraîche
20 g (¾ oz) lemon juice, plus extra to taste
60 g (2 oz) vegetable oil

Grapefruit blossom oil

20 g (¾ oz) grapefruit blossoms, stolen from your neighbour's tree
100 g (3½ oz) vegetable oil

To serve

¼ head of frisée
30 g (1 oz) pistachio nuts
8 large asparagus spears
15 g (½ oz) lemon juice
40 g (1½ oz) hard goat's feta

Buttermilk sauce

You really need to make this sauce as quickly as possible. If you blend the buttermilk for too long it will get warm and then it is near impossible to get the fluffy, airy consistency that makes it so cool. With this in mind, place the cold buttermilk, mustard, crème fraîche and lemon juice into a tall measuring jug. Using a hand-held blender, blend on high speed, slowly adding the oil until you form a thick and smooth texture. Season with salt and more lemon juice to taste.

Grapefruit blossom oil

Place the blossoms and oil into a small glass jar and close the lid. Turn your oven to 50°C (122°F), or the lowest setting, and place the jar inside. Gently warm for 1 hour. Turn the oven off and leave to cool in the oven overnight.

To serve

Using your hands, pick away any overly bitter or damaged outer leaves from the frisée. Wash thoroughly under cold running water to remove any unwanted visitors. Roughly chop the pistachios. Cut the tough base off of each asparagus spear then lightly oil and season. Quickly cook the spears over a hot grill or barbecue until only just cooked, about 1½ minutes. Remove from the fire and cut each spear into three pieces. Place into a mixing bowl with the frisée and pistachios. Dress with some of the grapefruit blossom oil and lemon juice, season to taste with salt and black pepper and give it a quick toss. Scoop a couple of spoons of the buttermilk sauce into the bottom of a serving bowl, cover with the salad mix and, finally, crumble the feta over the top.

Cherries, shiso, yuzu and salted coconut ice cream

How good are cherries? The idea here is a refreshing, multifaceted dessert that showcases the different dimensions cherries have to offer. By blending the fruit with some of the pits, we bring out some bitter almond notes to offset the sweetness. Coconut always goes great with cherries, and the yuzu skin adds another level of brightness.

Salted coconut ice cream

50 g (1¾ oz) liquid glucose

35 g (1¼ oz) sugar

100 g (3½ oz) fresh coconut water

140 g (5 oz) coconut cream

Whole cherry granita

600 g (1 lb 5 oz) cherries

100 g (3½ oz) sugar

Cherry jam

250 g (9 oz) cherries

125 g (4½ oz) sugar

zest and juice of ½ lemon

1 star anise

Crystallised purple shiso

2 egg whites

8 purple shiso leaves

100 g (3½ oz) sugar

To finish

150 g (5½ oz) cherries

10 g (¼ oz) preserved yuzu skin,
    sliced

Salted coconut ice cream

Place the glucose and sugar in a small pot with 70 g (2½ oz) water and warm over a low heat until the sugar dissolves. Pour the coconut water and cream into a medium-sized jug, then add the dissolved sugars and blend with a hand-held blender until smooth. Season to taste with salt, then freeze in an ice-cream machine according to the manufacturer's instructions.

Whole cherry granita

Using a hand-held pitting tool, remove the pits from each cherry, making sure you cover yourself because this will make a mess! Keep 20 g (¾ oz) of the pits and place them in an upright blender with the cherries, sugar and 500 g (1 lb 2 oz) water. Blend on high speed for around 3 minutes, or until you feel like the pits have definitely broken up nicely. Pour the mix into a container, chill for an hour, then strain through a fine-mesh sieve. Pour into a low-sided container and freeze solid, a minimum of 4 hours. When firm, scrape into a granita using a fork and keep in the freezer.

Cherry jam

Using the same hand-held pitting tool as above, pit the cherries and then cut them in half. Put the cherry halves, sugar, lemon and star anise into a small pot with 30 g (1 oz) water and warm over a low heat until the sugar dissolves and the cherries begin to release some of their liquid. At this point turn up the heat and cook until the liquid reduces to a thick, jammy consistency. Remove from the heat, get rid of the star anise and set aside to cool.

Crystallised purple shiso

Put the egg whites in a small bowl and, using either a small whisk or a fork, give them a quick whip to break down the whites to a free-flowing liquid. Take each shiso leaf and, working one by one, brush each side with the egg white, then lightly sprinkle with sugar. Place each sugared leaf onto a dehydrator rack and dry for at least 4 hours. If you don't have a dehydrator, place dry them in the oven on the lowest temperature you can muster. It can help to spray the rack very lightly with a cooking oil, then wipe off any excess oil with a paper towel. This will add a thin layer of insurance that is much needed so your leaves don't tear when it comes to removing them.

To finish

Using the hand-held pitting tool, pit each of the cherries, cut them in half and put them into a small mixing bowl. Add a spoon or two of the cherry jam and the yuzu skin and mix until combined. Take four small serving bowls and divide the cherry mix between them. Next, scoop in a generous chunk of the salted coconut ice cream. Take two of the shiso crisps and poke them into the ice cream so they stand up then spoon over the granita.

A trout fishing Sunday

Each year, at the beginning of November, my father, brother and I hike into the New Zealand high country to spend a few days fly fishing. It's something we've done for years now and it is one of those rare times we're all together and completely off-grid. There's no mobile reception, no people and, apart from the mosquitos and some epic views, nothing to distract us from trying to catch (and release) as many trout from the crystal clear water as we can.

In New Zealand it's illegal to sell trout, even in restaurants, so it's a privilege to be able to serve it here in Australia. This menu is a celebration of doing just that.

Serves 4

(1)   Pickled mussel toasts

(2)   Goat's curd, fennel, braised broad beans

(3)   Whole trout, mandarin, café de Melbourne butter

(4)   Wild rocket, hazelnut and parmesan

ON SUNDAYS

Pickled mussel toasts

At Embla, we serve this dish at three different temperatures, and you should too. The focaccia is toasted to order so it's lovely and warm. The rouille, which gives the dish its big notes of capsicum (bell pepper) and much of its brightness, is spooned on at room temperature. Lastly, the pickled mussels are laid on top straight out of the fridge because who would want a warm pickled mussel?

Fermented pepper rouille

2 eggs
90 g (3 oz) carrot
1 garlic clove, peeled
½ teaspoon chilli powder
15 g (½ oz) Dijon mustard
1 teaspoon smoked paprika
50 g (1¾ oz) Fermented
    pepper paste (see page 117)
60 g (2 oz) olive oil
lemon juice, to taste

Pickled mussels

1 kg (2 lb 3 oz) small mussels
20 g (¾ oz) vegetable oil
¼ fennel bulb, finely diced
2 garlic cloves, finely diced
sherry vinegar, to taste

To finish

30 g (1 oz) Fermented fennel pulp
    (see page 225)
5 g (⅛ oz) bronze fennel
    leaves, chopped
200 g (7 oz) focaccia
olive oil, for grilling

Fermented pepper rouille

Bring a small saucepan of water to the boil, add the eggs and simmer for 9 minutes. Run the eggs under cold water until they're cool enough to handle. Peel the shell away and then remove the cooked yolk and place in an upright blender. You can eat the boiled whites – they make a great chef's snack. Take the carrot and cut it into smallish dice, cover with water in a small pot and cook until tender. Drain and add to the blender along with 1 tablespoon water and all the other ingredients, except the olive oil. Blend on high until the mix is smooth, then slowly add the oil until emulsified. Season to taste with sea salt and lemon juice.

Pickled mussels

Bring a pot of water to a simmer and place a colander inside a bowl for the cooked mussels. Working in three or four batches, quickly blanch the mussels in the simmering water just until the shells crack open, then remove and place into the colander to drain. Once you have blanched all the mussels, refrigerate to chill. Reserve the liquid that collects at the bottom of the bowl and a little of the blanching water. Place the vegetable oil, fennel and garlic in a clean pot and sweat gently over a low heat until softened. Strain the mussel liquor through a fine-mesh sieve and add to the fennel pot. Bring this to the boil, skim well and simmer until you are happy with the flavour intensity. Pass the liquid through a fine sieve again and chill. Once cold, add the mussels and season to taste with sherry vinegar.

To finish

When you're ready to serve, drain the liquid from the mussels and carefully cut each mussel in half. Place them into a small bowl with the fennel pulp and chopped leaves and mix lightly. Using a bread knife, cut the focaccia into four 1 cm (½ in) thick finger-length slices. Lightly oil the cut faces with olive oil and grill on a barbecue until golden and crisp on the outside but still soft in the middle. Scoop half a tablespoon of pepper rouille on top and place four mussel halves on top.

Goat's curd, fennel, braised broad beans

The beauty of this dish – and a reason to make it in spring – is the new-season broad beans braised in their more tender outer pods. Not only is this way less of a drag than blanching and double-podding them, but you also get more bean per bean, if that makes sense. The fermented fennel juice supercharges your umami and can be made following the steps on page 225. It's a staple ingredient at Embla.

Goat's curd

120 g (4½ oz) home-made ricotta
(see page 32)

90 g (3 oz) goat's curd

5 g (⅛ oz) parmesan, finely grated

Braised broad beans

250 g (9 oz) young broad beans,
podded once

100 g (3½ oz) banana shallots, diced

50 g (1¾ oz) garlic cloves, sliced

100 g (3½ oz) olive oil

125 g (4½ oz) Fermented fennel juice
(see page 225)

10 g (¼ oz) thyme leaves

1 bay leaf

25 g (1 oz) parsley, leaves only

50 g (1¾ oz) broad bean leaves

20 g (¾ oz) fennel leaves,
chopped

lemon juice, to taste

Goat's curd

Place everything into a smallish bowl and mix to combine. Season the taste with sea salt.

Braised broad beans

Using a sharp knife, give the broad beans a little chop through. Ideally you only want to cut them in half, so don't get carried away. In a smallish pot gently sweat off the shallot and garlic over a low heat with a touch of the olive oil for 4 minutes. Once partially softened add the rest of the oil, fennel juice, broad beans, thyme, bay leaf and a good pinch of salt. Make sure that the beans are submerged and simmer very gently over a low heat until soft and army green. At this point add the parsley and leaves, stir through and remove from the heat. Let this cool and season to taste with sea salt, black pepper and a little lemon juice if needed. This tastes much better the following day.

To serve

Scoop the goat's curd onto a serving dish and, using the back of your spoon, make a large hole in the centre. Scoop a load of the braised broad bean mix into the centre and serve.

Whole trout, mandarin, café de Melbourne butter

Café de Melbourne butter is our take on the classic Paris original. Ours features ingredients that reflect Melbourne's diversity: cumin from the Middle East, oxidative sherry from Spain, Italian capers and oregano, and so on, as well as a hit of house-made vinegar created from Melbourne Bitter – which is well worth the effort of making, if you're that way inclined. You're going to spread this on a beautiful butterflied trout, which, by the way, is illegal to sell in New Zealand. It's a pleasure to be able to serve this on my menu.

Café de Melbourne butter

100 g (3½ oz) white wine

75 g (2¾ oz) oxidative sherry, such as Olorosso or Amontillado

7 g (¼ oz) fenugreek seeds

500 g (1 lb 2 oz) butter, softened

125 g (4½ oz) Fermented tomato paste (see page 117)

30 g (1 oz) capers

35 g (1¼ oz) Dijon mustard

75 g (2¾ oz) shallots, diced

2 garlic cloves, chopped

10 g (¼ oz) smoked paprika

3 g (¹⁄₁₀ oz) rosemary leaves, chopped

zest of 2 lemons

3 g (¹⁄₁₀ oz) cumin seeds, toasted

3 g (¹⁄₁₀ oz) dried oregano

5 g (⅛ oz) salt

10 g (¼ oz) sherry vinegar or Melbourne Bitter vinegar

1 g (¹⁄₃₂ oz) black peppercorns

100 g (3½ oz) hazelnuts

To finish

10 g (¼ oz) vegetable oil

2 × 350 g (12½ oz) rainbow trout, butterflied and bones removed

25 g (1 oz) orange juice

Café de Melbourne butter

In a small pot reduce the white wine, sherry and fenugreek by one third. Strain and chill. Place all of the remaining ingredients, plus the reduction, into a blender and pulse until combined. Season to taste.

To finish

If you have never butterflied a fish, it is a skill well worth learning. If you are time- or motivation-deficient then you can also ask you fishmonger to do this for you. Ideally you are going to want a wood-fired oven for this one, sitting around 500°C (932°F). Failing that you could turn your oven to the highest grill (broiler) fan-forced setting it can muster.

Lightly oil a cast-iron pan that's wide enough to hold the trout. Season the underside of the fish and place, skin side up, in the pan. Slather with a layer of room-temperature Café de Melbourne butter. Cook in the wood oven for around 1½ minutes, preferably in a spot where the flame will blast over the top of the fish. The key here is fast; the trout will cook quickly and in that short time you want to give the skin some texture and caramelisation. Remove from the oven and season with the orange juice, then transfer to a suitable plate to serve.

Wild rocket, hazelnut and parmesan

The secret here is to find real rocket that's grown outside in the sun. Buy it from a farmer. Pick it if you have to. Chefs are often accused of being unreasonably particular. Sometimes fairly. Mostly though, we just want you to have the best food experiences available, and full-flavoured, non-supermarket rocket is worth the extra effort.

Wild rocket pesto
75 g (2¾ oz) wild rocket (arugula)
1 garlic clove, peeled
50 g (1¾ oz) hazelnuts, toasted
40 g (1½ oz) parmesan, grated
125 g (4½ oz) olive oil
125 g (4½ oz) grapeseed oil

To finish
200 g (7 oz) wild rocket leaves

Wild rocket pesto

Place all of the ingredients in a small bowl blender and blitz until smooth, season with sea salt.

To finish

In a suitable bowl dress the rocket leaves with the rocket pesto, being careful to not add too much. Season to taste and mix gently.

A first barbecue
of the year Sunday

Weather wise, you can sometimes go too early with your first barbecue of the season, especially in the southern states (or where I'm from in New Zealand). But what I take from that is there's a kind of spiritual urge to grill outside, and it's not just the bearded blokes in the black rubber gloves who feel it. Grill smoke doesn't just smell great, it signals that good times are back again.

When cooking outside with fire, it's easy to get lost in a torpor of meat and bone. Here we're breaking it up with crunchy textures and citrusy highs to keep the meat sweats at bay.

Serves 4

(1) John Dory rillettes, blossom, capers, witlof

(2) Asparagus, goat's milk, goat's cheese

(3) Lamb, peas, shoots, chamomile

(4) Yoghurt semifreddo, fermented elderflower honey

ON SUNDAYS

John Dory rillettes, blossom, capers, witlof

Rillettes make a lot of sense in spring. They're shareable. You serve them cold. They play great off crisp and peppery new season leaves. On the other hand, spring is often not a time of year you want to be slow cooking pork submerged in fat, which is why we've subbed in a fillet of John Dory instead. This is a classic Embla starter that's luscious and rich but also fresh and light.

John Dory rillettes

1 fillet from a 1.5 kg (3 lb 5 oz) John Dory
juice of 1 lemon, plus zest of ½ lemon
25 g (1 oz) Aioli (page 225)
50 g (1¾ oz) olive oil

To finish

20 g (¾ oz) lemon blossom oil (made using the same technique as the Grapefruit blossom oil on page 41)
20 g (¾ oz) capers, chopped
5 g (⅛ oz) dried capers
5 g (⅛ oz) chives, snipped
a little lemon zest
3 yellow witlof (Belgian endive)

John Dory rillettes

Preheat the oven to 160°C (320°F). Make sure the dory fillet is clean of any skin or bones. We're going to cook the fish 'en papillote' so place the dory on a piece of baking paper big enough to fold into an envelope around itself. Season the fish with a little salt, microplane over the zest of ½ lemon and give it a touch of olive oil. Wrap the package up tight and bake in the oven for around 12 minutes. Remove and open the packet to let the fish cool. Once cool, place the fish in a small bowl and shred by hand, then mix in the aioli, remaining oil and 75 g (2¾ oz) water. Season to taste with salt and lemon juice, chill.

To finish

Scoop the rillettes into a pile in the centre of a steep-sided serving bowl. Over the top of the rillettes add the lemon oil, capers, chives and a little lemon zest. Cut the leaves of the witlof away from their roots and arrange around the edge of the bowl.

Asparagus, goat's milk, goat's cheese

Asparagus and goat's cheese go so well together that sometimes I imagine happy goats frolicking around with stumpy asparagus spears for horns. It's an easy image to conjure and that's got to count for something. Monte Enebro is an excellent goat's cheese that's handmade by a retired steel salesman and his daughter in Avila, Spain, which may be a cuter image than the asparagus-horned goats.

Goat's milk sauce

150 g (5½ oz) goat's milk
10 g (¼ oz) Dijon mustard
20 g (¾ oz) crème fraîche
5 g (⅛ oz) chardonnay vinegar
5 g (⅛ oz) lemon juice
60 g (2 oz) grapeseed oil

To finish

12 fat asparagus spears
vegetable oil
50 g (1¾ oz) Monte Enebro
   goat's cheese
lemon juice, to serve

Goat's milk sauce

Place everything except the oil into a small jug and blend until smooth with a hand-held blender. Slowly add the oil while blending until the sauce is nicely emulsified, then season to taste with sea salt.

To finish

Take the asparagus and oil lightly then season with salt. Over a very hot fire, grill the spears for 30 seconds on both sides. Scoop a couple of spoons of the goat's milk sauce onto a serving plate. Squeeze a little lemon juice over the asparagus then arrange on top of the sauce. Using a microplane, finely grate the cheese over the top.

ON SUNDAYS

Lamb, peas, shoots, chamomile

Tender spring peas and tender spring lamb cooked directly over hot coals. Fat – rendered out by the slow heat – drips onto the fire, scorching the meat and amping up that beautiful caramelised crust. (Side note: you're going to smell great after cooking this.) A lemon and chamomile-driven sauce, bolstered with chicken stock, adds a cut-through moreishness.

Lamb leg

20 g (¾ oz) each of rosemary, parsley, oregano leaves
3 garlic cloves, peeled
100 g (3½ oz) olive oil
1 lamb leg, boned

Chamomile oil

10 g (¼ oz) dried chamomile
100 g (3½ oz) vegetable oil

To finish

300 g (10½ oz) chicken stock
½ garlic clove, sliced
3 slices preserved Meyer lemons
150 g (5½ oz) fresh peas
100 g (3½ oz) pea shoots

Lamb leg

Make a marinade the night before by blending the herbs, garlic and oil together in an upright blender until smooth. Place the lamb in a suitably sized dish, coat with the marinade and chill overnight. The next day, light a nice fire and let the wood burn down for 45 minutes or so until you have a decent bed of coals. Take the lamb out of the fridge when you light the fire and let it come to room temperature. Using your hands, remove most of the marinade and place the lamb onto a rack around 1 metre (3.2 feet) above the surface of the fire. Cook slowly for around 1¼ hours, or until it reaches 50°C (122°F) when tested with a cooking thermometer. The trick here is to manage the heat so that it is consistent but slow; the slower it cooks the more tender it will be. Remove from the fire and let it rest, covered, in a warm spot for 10 minutes.

Chamomile oil

Place the dried chamomile and oil in an upright blender. Blend on high speed for 4–5 minutes, or until the oil becomes hot to the touch. Pour everything into a small container and leave at room temperature overnight to infuse. The following day, strain the oil off the top of the sediment and chill.

To finish

Place the stock, garlic and Meyer lemon slices into a small pot and bring to the boil. Simmer until it has reduced by one-third then season well with sea salt. Add the peas and take off the heat. Dress the pea shoots with the chamomile oil and season lightly. Carve the lamb leg and arrange on a serving plate, spoon over the peas and some of the sauce, then top with the pea shoots.

Yoghurt semifreddo, fermented elderflower honey

Backyard barbecues call for desserts that are simple to make but also clean and light enough to reset your palate after a rich meat course. The inherent sharpness of frozen yoghurt fits the bill perfectly. It's also a brilliant way to use some of the Fermented elderflower honey from page 71.

Semifreddo
250 g (9 oz) Greek-style yoghurt
200 g (7 oz) cream
3 egg whites
140 g (5 oz) sugar
lemon juice, to taste

To finish
80 g (2¾ oz) pistachio nuts
50 g (1¾ oz) Fermented elderflower
honey (see page 71)

Semifreddo

Place the yoghurt in a bowl and beat until smooth. In another bowl, whisk the cream to soft peaks. Place the egg whites in the bowl of an electric mixer fitted with the whisk attachment. Mix on medium speed until the whites begin to foam, then slowly add the sugar. Once all of the sugar is incorporated, beat on high speed until firm and glossy. Using a rubber spatula, carefully fold the whipped cream into the yoghurt, and then the meringue into the mixture. Season to taste with lemon juice and then freeze in a suitably sized tray for at least 4 hours before serving.

To finish

Remove the semifreddo from the freezer and cut slices. Transfer to a serving plate and scatter with the pistachios, then spoon over the elderflower honey.

What to do with elderflowers?

If seasons had mascots, elderflowers would make a great one for spring. For most of the year, elder trees are hard to spot, which is strange because they're everywhere. Then spring happens and they burst into bloom, erupting into these fat flowerheads of creamy white petals and sending their strangely spicy perfume in all directions. And then they're gone, as quickly as they came.

I remember googling 'elderflower tree' to see what they looked like. This was back when I was still running the Matterhorn in Wellington. My idea was to pick a bunch and do some experimenting, but for ages I couldn't find a single one. It wasn't until spring that I finally saw one, then five, then dozens of them, all within walking distance of where I was living.

But despite being a fairly innocuous-looking plant (it's classed as a weed even though it's native to eastern parts of Australia), elderflower has a wickedly evocative flavour. You'll get subtle notes of lychee and pear, along with grape. Then there's the musky aroma with hints of honey and hay.

Anyway, when elderflowers are blooming, you can easily end up with tonnes of them. Making cordial with it is great, but there are heaps of other delicious and versatile things you can make. Here are four of them.

Tips for handling elderflowers:

- Never pick anything from lower than a dog can pee.

- Try to pick in the morning when the flowers have just opened. It's said this is when they are at their most floral.

- Pick your flowers into a mesh bag or basket. Picking into plastic will make the flowers sweat and go bad quickly.

- Don't leave too much of the main stalk on the flower head, as this can upset some people's stomachs when used in an infusion.

- Give each flower head a good tap to remove any small bugs.

- Make sure to leave some flowers behind to grow into elderberries later in the summer.

SPRING

Elderflower vinegar

150 g (5½ oz) elderflower flower heads
1 kg (2 lb 3 oz) white vinegar

Place the elderflowers in a clean and sterilised glass jar big enough to hold all the vinegar. Pour the vinegar into a pot and warm to 65°C (149°F). Carefully pour the vinegar into the jar, close the lid and leave to cool. Once opened keep in the refrigerator.

This vinegar brings a bright floral freshness to any salad dressing, is great in a fruit poaching liquid and brightens any gin and tonic.

Lemon and elderflower sherbet

1.5 kg (3 lb 5 oz) milk
75 g (2¾ oz) elderflower heads
300 g (10½ oz) sugar
300 g (10½ oz) lemon juice

In a pot, warm the milk to 70°C (158°F) then remove from the heat. Add the elderflower heads and leave to cool for 1 hour. Strain the milk into a clean container. Take a small amount of the milk and warm it in a small pot with the sugar until it has dissolved. Stir the sweetened milk into the infused milk, then add the lemon juice. Freeze using an ice-cream machine according to the manufacturer's instructions.

Fermented elderflower honey

200 g (7 oz) filtered water
800 g (1 lb 12 oz) raw
  unprocessed honey
150 g (5½ oz) elderflower heads

Place the water then honey into a clean sterilised glass jar. Using a clean metal spoon stir until the honey is smooth and has been thinned down by the water. Add the elderflower heads, mix to combine and close the lid. Keep in a spot that isn't too cold or too warm. Stir every day for the first week, then let it ferment for a minimum of 6 months. Once opened, keep refrigerated.

This ferment takes a long time but is well worth the wait. I've always found it good right in the depths of winter when you need a little reminder of those sunny summer days.

Elderflower liqueur

150 g (5½ oz) elderflower heads
1 lemon
1 kg (2 lb 3 oz) vodka
125 g (4½ oz) sugar

Place the elderflower heads in a clean sterilised glass jar that is big enough to fit the flowers and vodka. Using a vegetable peeler cut strips of zest from the lemon and place on top of the flowers. Pour in the vodka and make sure that everything is submerged under the liquid. Seal the lid and leave in a cool dark spot for 2 weeks. Give it a stir every few days and taste to see how it is progressing. When you are happy with how much flavour has been pulled out of the flowers strain the liquid through the finest strainer you have – a piece of muslin (cheesecloth) is great for this. Make a sugar syrup by heating the sugar and 100 g (3½ oz) water together until the sugar dissolves, then let it cool. Add enough syrup to the elderflower vodka to reach your preferred level of sweetness. Pour the liqueur into a bottle and store in a dark cool spot for another month or so. While the liqueur will be fine to drink when you first blend it together it very much benefits from ageing a further month or two.

A long Sunday barbecue

If there's anything better than a Sunday, it's a long summer Sunday. In your twenties the instinct is to exert yourself on Friday and Saturday, but unlocking the potential of a Sunday without the normal consequences is cheat code stuff. Wake up, get your fire lit early and make a day of it.

This menu slots nicely into that cluster of long weekends that start in Melbourne around October, but for maximum effect, save it for when the sun is properly back in action. This is a solid cook, and iffy weather that's windy or overcast can add to your cooking time as well as your anxiety. It should feel casual and fun, not like an episode of *Alone*.

Serves 4

(1) Spritz to drink while cooking

(2) Lamb tomahawk, peppers, almond and sourdough

(3) Marinated cherry tomatoes, bay leaf and pine nut

Spritz to drink while cooking

Can you even barbecue without a drink in one hand? And does that drink have to be a beer? This is one of the many spritzes we invented at home during lockdown, part of a long series of spritz o'clock creations. The fernet we use is bitter and botanical, while the gin is super fresh and botanical. Make it icy and find a big stick to poke coals with.

45 ml (1½ fl oz) dry gin
    (e.g. The Melbourne Gin Company)
30 ml (1 fl oz) Fernet Hunter
30 ml (1 fl oz) cucumber juice
cucumber slices
ice
elderflower tonic

Measure the gin, fernet and fresh cucumber juice into your serving glass. Add a generous slice of cucumber, a handful of ice and top with the tonic. Give it a gentle stir and find a nice sunny spot to stand near where the lamb is cooking.

Lamb tomahawk, peppers, almond and sourdough

We'll start by cooking the lamb racks over a pit before resting it and breaking it down into tomahawk-like sections. The reason I'm a fan of this cut is because it gives you tasty between-the-ribs bits, the eye at the base of the rib, which is super tender, and plenty of delicious crackly skin. The peppers, loaded with heaps of sherry vinegar acidity, add high notes and balance.

Cooking the lamb

1 × whole lamb middle, split down the spine into two long boned racks

vegetable oil

Continued next page →

Cooking the lamb

Set up your grill with a rack suspended around 1 metre (3.2 feet) away from where the bed of coals will lay. Remove the lamb from the fridge and light your fire. You are looking to create a coal base here so that the lamb isn't cooking the whole time over a new yellow flame. You will need to light your fire at least 45 minutes before you intend to start cooking. Very lightly rub the lamb with vegetable oil and season well with sea salt. Place, bone side down, on the suspended rack. Now comes the fun part. Ideally you want to cook the lamb at a temperature of 60–65°C (140–149°F) for 2½ hours or so. You will need to manage the heat that comes off your coal bed and add new wood when needed, making sure that you don't scorch the lamb with the flame off the new log. Holding your hand above the fire will give you a great understanding of where the hot and cooler spots are. This is all the more enjoyable with a spritz in one hand and a few tales told. Slow-cook the rack for around 2 hours with the bone side down. The purpose of this is that the heat will penetrate the bones and help cook through the thicker parts of the meat. Once you feel like the rack is mostly cooked through, flip it over, skin side down, and give it a decent blast to caramelise the skin side. When you're happy, pull the rack off, loosely cover the lamb with foil or a clean tea towel (dish towel) and let it rest for 10 minutes. Using a sharp knife, cut each rack away from the spine bone, then carve each tomahawk into portions by cutting straight between the rib bones.

Confit peppers

4 red capsicums (bell peppers)

600 g (1 lb 5 oz) olive oil

3 garlic cloves, peeled

50 g (1¾ oz) oregano leaves

20 g (¾ oz) rosemary leaves

Almond cream

100 g (3½ oz) blanched almonds

½ garlic clove, peeled

20 g (¾ oz) olive oil

40 g (1½ oz) vegetable oil

sherry vinegar, to season

To finish

150 g (5½ oz) sourdough, crusts removed

70 g (2½ oz) olive oil

100 g (3½ oz) Fermented tomato juice (page 225), or juice from freshly crushed tomatoes

sherry vinegar, to season

20 g (¾ oz) basil leaves

30 g (1 oz) almonds, toasted

Confit peppers

Take the capsicums (bell peppers) and grill them hard and fast over an open flame, turning as needed so they char evenly. This could be either a wood fire or a gas flame. Once charred all over, place them in a bowl and cover with biodegradable plastic wrap for 10 minutes. Peel and de-seed the peppers, tear the flesh into large strips and lay on a tray. Season lightly with sea salt and leave to cure for 1 hour. While the peppers are curing, place the olive oil, garlic and herbs in a small pot and warm to around 50°C (122°F) over a low heat, then remove and leave to infuse. Once the peppers are ready place them in the oil and reheat to 50°C (122°F). Cook until the peppers have softened all the way through. Remove from the heat and chill.

Almond cream

Preheat your oven to 180°C (350°F). Place the almonds on a baking tray and very lightly toast for 4 minutes – you don't want any colour. Place the almonds, garlic and 150 g (5½ oz) water in an upright blender. Blend on high until smooth then slowly add the oils. Once emulsified, season with sea salt and sherry vinegar.

To finish

Using your hands, tear the bread into bite-sized chunks and place in an ovenproof frying pan. Add 30 g (1 oz) of the olive oil, season well and toss to coat. Bake at 180°C (350°F) until the croutons are crisp on the outside but still a little soft inside. Remove the pan from the oven and push the croutons to one side. Remove the peppers from their oil add to the pan so that the residual heat takes the chill off them. Place a few scoops of the almond cream into a wide serving bowl. Add the fermented tomato juice and the rest of the olive oil to the pan, season with sea salt and black pepper. Toss everything gently, season with a little sherry vinegar then arrange on top of the almond cream. Scatter the basil leaves and toasted almonds over the top.

ON SUNDAYS

Marinated cherry tomatoes, bay leaf and pine nut

At the restaurant, we used to put a cut-to-order tomato salad on the menu every summer. But given that everyone loves summer tomatoes, we'd end up making it for every single table, which would drive us crazy by the end of January. This recipe is our solution to capturing the sharpness and brightness of tomatoes in a way that could be pre-made and plated straight from the fridge. One of my finer moments.

Burnt bay leaf oil

20 g (¾ oz) bay leaves

500 g (1 lb 2 oz) vegetable oil

10 g (¼ oz) salt

Marinated cherry tomatoes

500 g (1 lb 2 oz) mixed ripe
    cherry tomatoes

20 g (¾ oz) vegetable oil

To finish

30 g (1 oz) sourdough
    breadcrumbs, toasted

30 g (1 oz) pine nuts, toasted

30 g (1 oz) Aioli (page 225)

5 g (⅛ oz) olive oil

2 g (¹⁄₁₆ oz) dried oregano

white vinegar, to season

Burnt bay leaf oil

Place the bay leaves into a wide grill sieve and grill over a hot bed of coals. The trick here is to grill them a little unevenly; you want a range from bright green and fragrant all the way through to 'I have to blow out the burning bay leaf'. Immediately transfer the leaves to an upright blender and add the other ingredients. Blend on high speed until the oil reaches 60°C (140°F), or is hot when you hold your hand against the blender bowl. Pour into a container big enough to hold the oil and the tomatoes and leave to cool.

Marinated cherry tomatoes

Place the tomatoes in a bowl and pick through to make sure they're clean and free of debris. Add the oil and season with sea salt. Working in small batches, grill the tomatoes quickly over a really ripping fire, then take them off the heat. The key here is speed, as we aren't looking to cook them at all, we just want the skin to blister and crack open. Place the grilled tomatoes straight into the bay oil and chill overnight, ideally.

To finish

Place the sourdough crumbs, pine nuts, aioli and olive oil in a small bowl. Season lightly and stir to combine, then scoop this into a pile on one side of your serving bowl. Using a slotted spoon, scoop the cherry tomatoes from their marinade and place into a bowl. Add the dried oregano and season to taste with salt, pepper and white vinegar. Arrange the tomatoes and some of the dressing on the other side of the serving bowl.

A summer backyard
harvest Sunday

The satisfaction you get from tending a backyard veggie patch is tinged with a measure of stress. When, at long last, your garden erupts with an explosion of cucumbers, capsicums (bell peppers), tomatoes, and zucchinis (courgettes), the pressure to not let any of it go to waste is real. It's your hard-earned harvest, after all.

Produce swaps are a good way of managing your excess and getting back items you didn't have space to plant. You could simply give to friends and family, as long as you know that they won't fully appreciate the love and care that went into growing it all. Or you could host a bunch of Sunday lunches like the one below.

Serves 4

(1)   Soured cucumbers, feta and dill

(2)   Friggitello peppers, cumin, mint and pumpkin seed pesto

(3)   Clams, yellow peppers, chickpeas and basil

(4)   Heirloom tomatoes, horseradish, kombu and summer savoury

Soured cucumbers, feta and dill

There are four things that have been at Embla since the beginning: me, my business partner Christian, our legendary kitchenhand Tej, and this dish. It's too refreshing and satisfying to ever come off the menu. You may want to start dehydrating the dill a day before serving.

Soured cucumbers

4 Lebanese (short) cucumbers
35 g (1¼ oz) table salt
400 g (14 oz) white vinegar
100 g (3½ oz) champagne vinegar
70 g (2½ oz) sugar
25 g (1 oz) salt
½ onion, sliced
1 bay leaf
25 g (1 oz) dill
1 tablespoon caraway seeds, toasted

Feta cream

125 g (4½ oz) soft feta curds, drained
25 g (1 oz) milk

To serve

½ bunch of dill

Soured cucumbers

Give the cucumbers a good wash under cold running water. Mix the table salt with 500 g (1 lb 2 oz) water until the salt has dissolved. Cut each cucumber in half lengthways and submerge in the salt brine for 1 hour. While the cucumbers are brining you can make the pickle base. Place the remaining ingredients in a pot, give them a good stir to dissolve everything and heat to around 60°C (140°F). Remove from the heat and leave to cool. When everything is ready to go, place the cucumbers and the pickle base into a vacuum-pack bag and seal under high pressure. Chill for at least 4 hours before serving.

Feta cream

Place the feta in a small bowl and beat until smooth using a spatula. Slowly work in the milk until you reach a soft whipped-cream consistency. Pour into a container and chill to set. This will firm up again as it cools.

To serve

Place the dill, stems and all, onto a dehydrator tray and dry on a very low temperature overnight. You may be able to do this in an oven with its pilot light on overnight if you don't happen to have a dehydrator laying around. When completely dry, crush into a fine powder using a spice grinder or mortar and pestle. To serve, scoop a spoon or two of the feta cream onto a small plate. Pick the plate up and give it a good tap from underneath to flatten the cream out. Remove the cucumbers from their pickle and slice into 1 cm (½ in) cross-sections. Dust some of the dill powder around the plate and top with the sliced cucumbers.

SUMMER

Friggitello peppers, cumin, mint and pumpkin seed miso

These fast-fried, mild little peppers have a big green capsicum (bell pepper) flavour. And dusted with a cumin-based salt, they make incredible finger food. Here they're served on a base of pumpkin seed (pepita) miso, which gives a deep, savoury nuttiness. Some of the chilli heads out there may want to sub in something spicier, like Padrón peppers. Knock yourselves out.

Pumpkin seed miso

150 g (5½ oz) pumpkin seeds (pepitas)
30 g (1 oz) broad bean miso
 or white Japanese miso
75 g (2¾ oz) vegetable oil
15 g (½ oz) lemon juice

Spiced salt

2 tablespoons cumin seeds, toasted
½ teaspoon salt
1 teaspoon sesame seeds, toasted
1 tablespoon dried mint leaves

To finish

vegetable oil, for deep-frying
300 g (10½ oz) friggitello peppers

Pumpkin seed miso

Place the pumpkin seeds and miso in a small upright blender. Blend on high speed while adding 200 g (7 oz) water and the oil. Blend until smooth and it has a dipping consistency, then season with salt and lemon juice. Chill.

Spiced salt

In a mortar and pestle, grind the cumin and salt until fine. Add the sesame and mint and work until they have broken down slightly, but still have a resemblance of their former selves.

To finish

Heat enough oil for deep-frying in a saucepan and bring it up to 180°C (350°F). Working in two batches, fry the peppers for around 2 minutes per batch. You will need to move the peppers around while frying so that they cook evenly on all sides. When they look like they're about to soften, remove and place in a mixing bowl lined with paper towel. Drain for 30 seconds, remove the paper towel and sprinkle liberally with the spiced salt. Scoop a few generous spoons of the pumpkin seed miso into the bottom of a steep-sided serving bowl. Arrange the peppers around the outer edge then sprinkle a little more spiced salt over for good measure.

Clams, yellow peppers, chickpeas and basil

One of my favourite seafood and herb combinations is clams with basil. The brightness and floral notes of basil pair great with the sharp salinity of clams, which have an underrated richness, especially when you amp them up with some butter and pancetta.

30 g (1 oz) pancetta
35 g (1¼ oz) olive oil
300 g (10½ oz) clams
2 garlic cloves, sliced
100 g (3½ oz) Fish skin stock
    (page 225)
20 g (¾ oz) butter
2 g (¹⁄₁₆ oz) rosemary leaves, chopped
2 yellow banana peppers
100 g (3½ oz) chickpeas, cooked
6 basil leaves, plus 15 g (½ oz) basil,
    chopped
lemon juice, to taste

Ideally you want to cook this dish in a ripping hot wood-fired oven, somewhere around 500–550°C (932–1022°F) is good. Failing that, a good hot gas pizza oven or a very, very hot fan-forced conventional oven will do. Dice your pancetta into thin lardons and heat a wide cast-iron pan over a medium heat. Add 20 g (¾ oz) of the oil, then the pancetta, and cook for 3 minutes until the fat starts to render from the pork. Turn the heat right up and add all the remaining ingredients, except the 15 g (½ oz) chopped basil, remaining oil and lemon juice. Give everything a little toss to coat and place the pan into your oven. This will only take 4–6 minutes – just enough time for the clams to begin to open. Make sure to pull the pan out halfway through and give everything a quick stir to make sure it cooks evenly. When all of the clams have opened, remove and add the remaining basil, and olive oil and season with salt and lemon juice to taste.

ON SUNDAYS

Heirloom tomatoes, horseradish, kombu and summer savoury

It's strange to think about it, but the herbs we see at the grocer represent just a fraction of what's out there in the wild. Imagine all the flavours we've overlooked or forgotten about. Summer savoury is one such forgotten herb. Closely resembling rosemary with a hint of thyme, its complex and resin-y depth pairs amazingly with summer tomatoes.

Kombu oil

35 g (1¼ oz) dried kombu
200 g (7 oz) vegetable oil

Horseradish crème fraîche

125 g (4½ oz) crème fraîche
20 g (¾ oz) fresh horseradish

To finish

300 g (10½ oz) ripe heirloom tomatoes
40 g (1½ oz) Fermented tomato juice
   (page 225)
5 g (⅛ oz) summer savoury,
   finely chopped

Kombu oil

Place the kombu and oil in an upright blender. Blend on high speed until the oil reaches 65°C (149°F). Transfer to a container and leave at room temperature overnight to infuse. You will make more oil than you need for this recipe, but it will keep refrigerated.

Horseradish crème fraîche

Place the crème fraîche into a small mixing bowl. Using a microplane, grate the horseradish into the bowl. Give it a good mix and season with salt to taste.

To finish

Scoop the horseradish cream onto the middle of a serving plate. Using a sharp knife, cut the tomatoes into chunky wedges and place in a mixing bowl. Add the fermented tomato juice, 30 g (1 oz) kombu oil, the summer savoury and season well with salt and black pepper. Give it a gentle mix and check the seasoning. Arrange the tomatoes around the cream and spoon over some of the dressing.

A languid Sunday

There's something about using a tablecloth at lunch that feels way more sophisticated than it should. This seems especially true on a hot summer Sunday when you could just as easily be sinking burgers in some beer garden somewhere or eating fish and chips straight off the paper. I'm not sure I even owned a tablecloth at home until last year.

But the secret to eating off linen is being OK with the spills. You think the old-time aristocrats weren't messy eaters? Wanting to keep the table as pristine as a church altar is a middle-class urge that we can all dispense with. This menu is built for sharing, and spilling, and enjoying with great friends. In terms of the cooking, it's also deceptively simple, meaning more time for you at the table.

Serves 4

(1) Raw beef, ginger, finger lime

(2) Poached rainbow trout, sunflower seed,
       parsley and artichoke

(3) Roast turbot, fermented tomato sauce vierge

(4) Fig, figs, fig leaf

ON SUNDAYS

Raw beef, ginger, finger lime

Yes, if done right this will look like an uncooked burger. Contentious? We leaned into it, so hopefully it's at least a conversation starter. A tiny dice on the beef gives a luscious mouthfeel. Adding to the raw patty visual are sharp bursts of finger lime and shallot, which also bring brightness and balance.

Ginger oil
100 g (3½ oz) fresh ginger, peeled
200 g (7 oz) vegetable oil

To finish
160 g (5½ oz) beef rump
1 teaspoon finely diced shallot
3 tablespoons red finger lime

Ginger oil

Roughly chop the ginger and place in an upright blender with the veg' oil. Blend on high until the oil reaches 60°C (140°F). Transfer to a container and leave to infuse overnight. In the morning the solids will have settled to the bottom. Carefully pass the oil through a strainer and chill.

To finish

Place the beef into the freezer for around an hour, or until very firm but not frozen. Working quickly while the rump is firm, cut into 2 mm (¹⁄₁₆ in) dice. Place the diced rump into a mixing bowl, add the shallot and finger lime. Season with salt and add the ginger oil to taste. Place low ring moulds onto two plates and divide the mix between them. Using the back of a spoon, flatten it so that it resembles a macabre raw burger patty. Remove the moulds and serve.

Poached rainbow trout, sunflower seed, parsley and artichoke

This is a super satisfying way to cook fish. Milk's high fat content lets it absorb more flavour than wine or water, which in turn means you can get a lot more of your aromats (in this case garlic) into whatever you're poaching. But the most satisfying part is how nicely the trout skins peel back once they're done. There are no words to properly describe it.

Poached trout

1 × 1.4 kg (3 lb 1 oz) rainbow trout
500 g (1 lb 2 oz) skim milk
4 garlic cloves, peeled and sliced
10 g (¼ oz) salt

Sunflower seed cream

25 g (1 oz) sunflower seeds
12 g (½ oz) broad bean miso
    or white Japanese miso
40 g (1½ oz) vegetable oil

To finish

2 baby globe artichokes, prepped
    and submerged in lemon water
    (see page 27)
30 g (1 oz) Lemon dressing (page 225)
30 g (1 oz) parsley, leaves only

Poached trout

Break the trout down into two fillets, removing the bones but leaving the skin on. Place the fillets into a shallow heatproof tray with sides high enough to contain the milk. Put the milk, garlic and salt in a pot and bring to scalding point, or until tiny bubbles appear around the edge of the pot, then set aside for 10 minutes. Bring the milk mix up to a rolling boil and pour it through a fine-mesh sieve over the trout fillets. Make sure that they are mostly submerged then leave them to cook in the hot milk for 9 minutes. Give the tray a little shake halfway through to ensure the fillets haven't stuck to the bottom and that they cook evenly. When the timer is up, use a fish slice to very carefully transfer the trout to a dry tray. Here's the cool bit: using tweezers or your hands very carefully pull the skin away from the flesh, starting at the tail end. Chill the fillets.

Sunflower seed cream

Blend the seeds and miso in an upright blender then slowly add 125 g (4½ oz) water and the oil until combined. Season to taste with salt. Set out two serving plates and artistically spoon 2 tablespoons of the sunflower seed cream over each. One at a time, pick each cold trout fillet up and gently break in half using your hands, place the smaller tail segment on the bottom of one plate and the larger piece on top. Take a small mixing bowl and, using a sharp mandolin, shave the artichokes as finely as you can into the bowl. Add the lemon dressing and season with salt. Add the parsley leaves, stir through quickly and arrange three little piles around the trout in each dish.

SUMMER

ON SUNDAYS

Roast turbot, fermented tomato sauce vierge

Turbot looks like a big flounder, and both delicious fish share a kind of gelatinous richness. In other words, they can make your lips stick together, much like a properly made veal stock. It's decadent enough to call for a high acid accompaniment, and this take on a sauce vierge using fermented tomato juice fits the bill completely.

1 × 1.5 kg (3 lb 5 oz) whole turbot

2 ripe red tomatoes

20 g (¾ oz) vegetable oil

30 g (1 oz) white wine

125 g (4½ oz) Fermented tomato juice (page 225)

1 garlic clove, sliced

5 basil leaves

1 tablespoon chopped chervil

1 tablespoon snipped chives

1 tablespoon parsley leaves, chopped

40 g (1½ oz) olive oil

lemon juice, to taste

Remove your turbot from the fridge and let it come up to an ambient temperature. Preheat your wood-fire oven to around 450°C (842°F). Place a small pot of water on to boil. Lightly score the top and bottom of each tomato, quickly blanch and immediately plunge into ice-cold water. Remove the skin, cut away the seed core, then cut the flesh into small dice. When you are ready to cook the fish, set a cast-iron frying pan large enough to hold the fish over a medium–high heat. Add a little veg' oil to the pan and season the turbot with salt. Sear, skin side down, until the side takes on a little colour, then flip it over with the dark side up. Place the pan into your oven and cook for 6–9 minutes, depending on your fish and your oven. Check the internal temperature by inserting a metal skewer into the thickest part of the fish near the spine. Remove it and hold the skewer against the back of your hand, if it's hot then it is cooked enough. Remove the turbot from the pan and place onto a serving dish. Set the pan over a medium heat and add the wine then the tomato juice, garlic and basil. Let it simmer for 3 minutes, or until it is tasty and has reduced slightly. Finish the sauce by adding the diced tomatoes, remaining herbs and olive oil. Give it a good swirl and taste, season with a little salt and lemon juice. Spoon the sauce over the turbot and serve.

Fig, figs, fig leaf

It'd be cool to find out how much having an established fig tree in the backyard adds to the value of a house. Every summer I find myself keenly aware of how the neighbourhood figs are progressing, and more importantly, which ones are hanging far enough over fences. This dessert celebrates everything we love about peak figs – the luscious fruit itself as well as their underrated, almost coconut-flavoured leaves.

Fig leaf custard

25 g (1 oz) fresh fig leaves
400 g (14 oz) cream
140 g (5 oz) milk
60 g (2 oz) egg yolks
50 g (1¾ oz) sugar

Fig vinegar granita

10 g (¼ oz) sugar
200 g (7 oz) verjuice from white grapes
20 g (¾ oz) Fig-leaf vinegar (see page 225)

Fig caramel

200 g (7 oz) sugar
50 g (1¾ oz) dried figs, chopped

To finish

4 ripe figs

Fig leaf custard

Set your oven to 150°C (302°F). In a pot, warm the fig leaves, cream and milk to around 60°C (140°F). Leave to infuse for 30 minutes, then remove the fig leaves. In a small bowl, mix the yolks with the sugar. Add a ladle of the milk mix to the yolks to loosen, then add the yolks to the pot and stir carefully, taking care to not introduce too many bubbles at this point. Pour 150 g (5½ oz) of custard into each of your four ramekins, place the ramekins into a baking dish and fill with tap hot water to halfway up the ramekins. Cover the dish with foil and bake for around 40 minutes. You should be able to jiggle the custard and have the mix move like a homogenous wave. Remove and chill to set.

Fig vinegar granita

In a small pot, warm the sugar and 25 g (1 oz) water until the sugar has dissolved. Mix with the verjuice and vinegar and freeze solid in a shallow tray. Once solid, use a fork to scrape the ice into a granita.

Fig caramel

Place the sugar and 70 g (2½ oz) water into a small pot and cook to a golden caramel over a high heat. Remove from the heat and allow the sugar to slow down a little. After 2 minutes, carefully add 50 g (1¾ oz) water and swirl through. Add the chopped figs, mix through and leave to infuse for 1 hour. Give the caramel a really good stir to try to release the fig seeds, then pass through a coarse strainer. You want to remove the flesh and keep the seeds.

To finish

Remove the custards from the fridge, spoon 1 teaspoon of the fig caramel on top and swirl to cover. Using a sharp knife, cut the figs in half vertically then slice finely. Arrange the slices around the top of the custard like a fan. Scoop a good spoon of the granita on top and serve straight away.

A Sunday with seafood

When planning a seafood lunch, I think the natural instinct is to go with your classic finger bowl spread: prawns, crays and snapper or barramundi cooked whole. As delicious as that is, it can be a bit of work for the guests and you often end up with bins smelling like Port Melbourne's Station Pier at low tide.

Serves 4

(1)   Oysters with chardonnay vinegar ice

(2)   Raw kingfish, lemon cucumber, mint and cumquat

(3)   Baby octopus, fennel, chickpeas and black lemon

(4)   Sesame, peach, marigold, fermented osmanthus honey

ON SUNDAYS

Oysters with chardonnay vinegar ice

I started out not liking oysters, then one of my first bosses made me eat trays of them, which only made things worse. In my defence, the Bluff oysters we used to get back in New Zealand were always extremely dead by the time we got them. That said, if I ever wanted to eat one, this is how I'd do it: fresh, ice cold, and dressed with something sharp and bright. The granita here is made with Forvm, an incredible chardonnay vinegar, that we don't do much to besides freeze.

Chardonnay vinegar ice

20 g (¾ oz) sugar

100 g (3½ oz) Forvm chardonnay vinegar

To serve

12 oysters

ice

Chardonnay vinegar ice

Warm the sugar and 125 g (4½ oz) water together in a small pot to dissolve, then allow to cool. Add the vinegar and season to taste with salt. Freeze in a shallow container. Once solid, scrape with a fork to create a granita. Freeze a small bowl to serve the granita in.

To serve

Shuck the oysters and crush the ice. Lay the ice in a serving bowl and arrange the oysters around the outside. Scoop the vinegar ice into the frozen bowl and serve.

Raw kingfish, lemon cucumber, mint and cumquat

Kingfish is on the meatier end of the fish spectrum, so it pairs really well with the pepita miso. I love this dish. It's got a wicked balance of savoury and brightness. Citrus is my thing and cumquat is such an elegant flavour. Lemon cucumbers, though not sour, have an enticing lemon scent and taste great. To make the dried cucumber skin, dry out any excess cucumber peel over a fire or in a low oven then grind into a fine powder.

Pumpkin seed cream

30 g (1 oz) pumpkin seeds (pepitas)

10 g (¼ oz) broad bean miso or white Japanese miso

40 g (1½ oz) vegetable oil

lemon juice, to taste

Cumquat oil

25 g (1 oz) cumquat skins

25 g (1 oz) olive oil

75 g (2¾ oz) vegetable oil

Cumquat dressing

25 g (1 oz) cumquat juice

25 g (1 oz) lemon or plain shio koji (page 225)

50 g (1¾ oz) Cumquat oil (see above)

To serve

140 g (5 oz) kingfish, cleaned and cut into 5 mm (¼ in) dice

20 g (¾ oz) pumpkin seeds (pepitas), soaked in water overnight

5 g (⅛ oz) olive oil

120 g (4½ oz) lemon cucumbers, or heirloom cucumbers

5 g (⅛ oz) lemon basil

5 g (⅛ oz) mint

1 teaspoon dried cucumber skin, ground

Pumpkin seed cream

Blend the seeds and miso in an upright blender and slowly add 100 g (3½ oz) water and the oil. Season to taste with salt and lemon juice.

Cumquat oil

Put everything in a small glass jar and place into a 60°C (140°F) oven for 6 hours. Leave to cool overnight.

Cumquat dressing

Mix everything together and season to taste if needed.

To serve

Place the kingfish and drained pumpkin seeds in a small bowl. Add the olive oil and season lightly with salt and black pepper. Mix well and transfer to two serving bowls. Make a small hole in the middle of the piles of fish. Spoon 1½ spoons of the pepita cream into the hole. Using a sharp knife, cut the cucumbers on an angle 4 mm (¼ in) thick. Place in a mixing bowl. Tear the herbs roughly with your hands and add to the bowl with the cucumber powder. Season lightly and dress with the cumquat dressing. Mix and arrange on top of the kingfish mix.

ON SUNDAYS

Baby octopus, fennel, chickpeas and black lemon

The unsung hero in this dish is the green chilli. It lends a vibrant herbiness without any heat. When cooking octopus you want to go low and slow or fast and hard. Here, we're going fast and hard, which will have your octopus coming out tender but with bite. The chickpea mix, with its fermented fennel juice, might just ruin all other chickpea dishes for you.

Black lemons
2 lemons

Octopus marinade
2 garlic cloves, minced
3 g ($\frac{1}{10}$ oz) fennel seeds, toasted
2 g ($\frac{1}{16}$ oz) coriander seeds, toasted
0.5 g ($\frac{1}{32}$ oz) ground black pepper
2 g ($\frac{1}{16}$ oz) salt
50 g (1¾ oz) vegetable oil
1 g ($\frac{1}{32}$ oz) rosemary leaves, chopped
250 g (9 oz) baby octopus, cleaned

To finish
½ garlic clove, finely sliced
200 g (7 oz) chickpeas, cooked
150 g (5½ oz) Fermented fennel juice (see page 225)
50 g (1¾ oz) fennel bulb, finely diced and blanched
1 tablespoon finely diced green chilli
20 g (¾ oz) butter
lemon juice, to taste
Aioli (page 225), to serve

Black lemons

You can buy black lemons from a Middle Eastern grocer, but they won't be quite the same. To make them at home, try to buy lemons that haven't been waxed or, failing this, give them a good wash under hot water. Place the lemons into a rice cooker and keep on warm mode for 1 month. Once the lemons have turned a deep black, remove them and dry over a fire until completely dried out and firm, around 3–4 days. Otherwise, you can dry them in a dehydrator for the same length of time. Roughly smash the dried lemons and grind into a fine powder using a spice grinder.

Octopus marinade

Place everything in a bowl and mix with your hands until the octopus is evenly coated. Marinate overnight.

To finish

You ideally want to cook the octopus in a wood-fired oven. Failing that, they are delicious grilled over a wood fire. In a small pot put the garlic, chickpeas, fennel juice and blanched fennel. Bring to a boil and simmer for 4 minutes. To finish, stir in the chilli and butter. Season with salt and lemon juice to taste.

In a cast-iron skillet, quickly blast the baby octopus in the wood oven. They will only take 2 minutes to cook through and will need to be flipped over halfway. Divide the chickpea mix between two bowls then add a scoop of aioli. Arrange the octopus on top and sprinkle with a little black lemon powder.

Sesame, peach, marigold, fermented osmanthus honey

There's no real name for this and for a while we were calling it 'Cloud'. It's sort of like a parfait or semifreddo but more delicate and much lighter. In fact, it's insanely light and, for want of a shorter word, voluminous. Put a big fluffy spoon into your mouth and it melts down to nothing. Magic. The fermented honey is super luxurious, flavoured with apricot-tasting osmanthus flowers.

Sesame semifreddo

250 g (9 oz) cream

20 g (¾ oz) white sesame seeds, toasted

50 g (1¾ oz) white chocolate

5 egg whites

100 g (3½ oz) sugar

To finish

2 ripe peaches, peeled, destoned and diced

40 g (1½ oz) Fermented osmanthus flower honey (see page 225)

2 ripe peaches, peeled, destoned, diced and dried in a very low oven overnight

5 g (⅛ oz) dried marigold flowers

Sesame semifreddo

Bring the cream up to 80°C (176°F) in a small pot. Add the sesame and chocolate. Mix until the chocolate has melted then set aside to infuse for 1 hour. Strain off the sesame seeds and chill overnight. The following day, whip the sesame chocolate cream to soft peaks in a bowl. Place the egg whites into the bowl of a stand mixer fitted with a whisk attachment. Combine the sugar and 40 g (1½ oz) water in a small pot and cook through to 117°C (243°F). While the sugar is cooking, turn the mixer on and start whipping the whites. When the sugar reaches temperature, turn the speed right up on the mixer and slowly pour in the sugar until incorporated. Whisk until cool and then fold this meringue into the whipped sesame cream. Gently transfer to a container, cover and freeze for at least 6 hours.

To finish

Divide the fresh peach between the bottom of two serving bowls. Using a spoon, cut a large chunk out of the semifreddo and place on top of the peach. Spoon some of the osmanthus honey over the top, scatter some of the dried peach over that, then finish with the dried marigold petals.

Preserving your summer veg' bounty

I've been working on the theory that – bear with me – pickling is a lot like photography. Taking a great picture is about capturing a passing moment in time so that you can enjoy it even after the moment has gone. The same can be said for taking a glut of produce at the peak of its season – the product of a complex, unrepeatable combination of climatic factors – and preserving its key characteristics.

Both of these things take a measure of thoughtfulness. Just like a photograph calls for composition and a balance of light and dark, your pickles should also be made in a way that highlights what you're most trying to capture. If you can't tell, I've recently taken up photography, but I think the theory holds.

I've spoken about my mum's cooking, she used to pickle and preserve all manner of veggies and fruits (which spurred my love of jarred fruit on ice cream), but in spite of that, it wasn't until I trained as a chef that I learned to do it myself. This says a fair bit about how pickling has gone from a necessity to something quite the opposite. But if you're someone who grows their own veggies, is good at finding beautiful market produce, or even if you're neither of those things but you know your way around a camera, pickling is a skill well worth picking up.

Preserved peppers

2 garlic cloves

750 g (1 lb 11 oz) olive oil

2 kg (4 lb 6 oz) mixed capsicums (peppers) of your choice

2 bay leaves

5 g (⅛ oz) rosemary leaves

15 g (½ oz) oregano leaves

Preheat your wood-fired oven to 450°C (842°F). Place the garlic in an ovenproof pan, cover and slowly roast in the coldest corner of your oven until soft and caramelised. Cool, then peel away any skin. Lightly oil your peppers and grade them by size, so that they will cook at an even rate. Working in batches, put the peppers in a cast-iron pan and blast them in the wood oven close to the coal base. The trick here is to char them quickly but not cook them through too much. Remove them from the oven and leave to cool slightly. Pull the stems off and remove as many of the seeds as you can. Take a sterilised glass preserving jar and, working one by one, season each pepper with salt and layer into the jar. As you go add the herbs evenly as well as the olive oil. Finally, cover with a final layer of olive oil and seal with a lid. Grab a pot large enough to cover the top of your jar by 10 cm (4 in) and place a small rack on the base of it. Fill the pot three-quarters full with water and bring to a simmer. Very gently lower the jar onto the rack at the base of the pot and simmer for 10 minutes. Remove the jar and upend it onto its lid. Leave to cool. Keep in the fridge once opened.

Fermented tomato paste

1 kg (2 lb 3 oz) ripe tomatoes, or capsicums (bell peppers)

20 g (¾ oz) salt

50 g (1¾ oz) whey from a naturally cultured yoghurt or previously fermented juice

Using a knife, roughly chop the tomatoes and place into a bowl blender. Blend for a minute or so until the tomatoes break down into a coarse puree. Transfer everything to a large vacuum-pack bag, then add the salt and whey. Give it a good shake, then vacuum on high pressure in a vacuum sealer. Leave the bag at room temperature for 3 weeks. During this time the fermentation will develop and begin to create gas within the bag, normally around day five. You will need to burp the bag of this gas and re-vac it several times. Believe me, these things explode and make a hell of a mess, especially when kept on a high shelf. When the tomato juice is sour enough to your liking, it can be kept as a juice in the fridge to stop any further development. To make a paste, semi-dry the juice using a dehydrator overnight, or in a low oven over a few hours. This paste is an excellent turbo booster for anything from pasta to a beef sauce.

Pickled black walnuts

100 g (3½ oz) salt

1 kg (2 lb 3 oz) green walnuts

200 g (7 oz) honey

1 kg (2 lb 3 oz) malt vinegar

4 bay leaves

10 g (¼ oz) black peppercorns

15 g (½ oz) coriander seeds

Take a medium-sized bucket and add 2 kg (4 lb 6 oz) water and the salt. Give it a good stir to dissolve. Using a fine cake-testing pin, carefully stab each walnut 3–4 times. This will help the brine penetrate during the fermentation stage. Place the walnuts into the brine and weigh them down with a plate so that the nuts are submerged under the liquid. Put the bucket somewhere cool, like a wine room, for a week to ferment. This will help leech out some of the astringency from the walnuts. After a week, drain the walnuts off, cover with a fresh brine and ferment for another week. Drain off the brine and lay the walnuts in a single layer on a tray. Leave them to dry out and oxidise at room temperature overnight. This will turn them from a dark army green to a deep jet black – pretty cool! Place the honey, vinegar, bay leaves and spices in a pot and warm just enough to dissolve the honey, then season with a healthy slug of salt. Transfer the walnuts to a sterilised jar that fits in your fridge and pour over the pickling liquid. Make sure the walnuts are submerged fully, cover with a lid and refrigerate for a minimum of 3 months.

Preserved zucchini

5 kg (11 lb) zucchini (courgettes)

170 g (6 oz) salt

425 g (15 oz) white vinegar

425 g (15 oz) champagne vinegar

2 kg (4 lb 6 oz) olive oil

4 garlic cloves, peeled

1 bunch of oregano

Set yourself up with either two buckets the same size or, failing that, two medium bowls the same size. They will need to fit in your fridge. Wash the zucchini under cold running water. Using a mandolin, cut the zucchini into 1.5 mm (1/16 in) thin discs. Make sure you watch out for your fingertips! Place the sliced zucchini into a large bowl and sprinkle over the salt. Give it a thorough mix with your hands, then transfer to one of your buckets. Place the second bucket inside the first and fill with about 2 litres (68 fl oz) water. This is intended to press the zucchini reasonably firmly, and the general rule of thumb here is an equal weight of pressure to zucchini. Put this all into the fridge overnight. The following day, drain off all the liquid from the zucchini and pour both of the vinegars into the bucket. Mix well then weigh down again with the second bucket and chill overnight again. Add the olive oil to a pot with the garlic and oregano. Warm to around 45°C (113°F) over a low heat, then remove and leave to cool to room temperature. Drain the vinegar off the zucchini and, working with your hands, squeeze handfuls of zucchini reasonably firmly to remove any excess liquid. Place into a sterilised jar and cover with the infused olive oil. These will keep refrigerated for months.

(3)   Autumn

A meat-free Sunday

When eating with a vegetarian, avoid asking how long they've been that way because the only logical next question is, 'Why did you stop eating meat?'. Chances are their answer will make it difficult for you to continue enjoying your non-vegetarian meal and, more importantly, why put people on the spot in the first place?

I suppose that's just one example of how we meat eaters can feel awkward around our non-meat-eating friends. Another good one is when we're the ones cooking. Not being able to use the usual bag of tricks is hard. But it helps to remember that the key component missing from a lot of vegetarian dishes isn't actually meat – it's umami. And that's something the following recipes have in spades.

Serves 4

(1)   Stracciatella, walnut and cime di rapa

(2)   Grilled English spinach, green olive and oregano

(3)   Braised escarole, garlic and Espelette bucatini

(4)   Raw quince ice cream, honeycomb and nashi pear

Stracciatella, walnut and cime di rapa

Cime di rapa, also known as broccoli rabe in the northern hemisphere, is a leafy, big-tasting plant with strong mustard and turnip-y notes. The stems can be stringy, but when peeled and cooked at a low heat, they wilt into the most delicious addition to any pizza or pasta. Keep some covered in olive oil at the back of your fridge and you'll be surprised how much you use it.

Braised cime di rapa

300 g (10½ oz) cime di rapa

1 garlic clove, finely sliced

15 g (½ oz) oregano, leaves only

small pinch of Espelette chilli flakes

100 g (3½ oz) olive oil

Black walnut pesto

75 g (2¾ oz) walnuts

50 g (1¾ oz) Pickled black walnuts (page 117)

1 garlic clove, peeled

10 g (¼ oz) parmesan

50 g (1¾ oz) olive oil

25 g (1 oz) vegetable oil

To finish

150 g (5½ oz) fresh stracciatella curds

crostini, to serve

Braised cime di rapa

Give the cime di rapa a good wash under cold running water and gently shake dry. Pick the leaves and flower heads into a suitably sized bowl. Take the stems and, using the tip of a small paring knife, peel away the fibrous outer layer starting from the base and working up. When peeled, finely slice the stems on the diagonal. Place all of the ingredients into a suitably sized pot, season with a little salt and cook over a low–medium heat until softened. This will take around 15 minutes – you want the rapa to turn an even army green and become luxuriously soft in texture. When it is ready, remove from the heat, leave to cool then season to taste with salt and black pepper.

Black walnut pesto

Preheat the oven to 180°C (350°F). Place the fresh walnuts on a baking tray and toast for 3–4 minutes. You do not want to brown them much at all, just toast some of the rawness off them. Remove from the oven and leave to cool. Using a sharp knife, roughly chop the toasted nuts, followed by the black walnuts. Transfer the nuts to a small mixing bowl and microplane in the parmesan followed by a touch of garlic (start with half a small clove, you can always add more afterwards). Pour in the oils, give it a good mix and season to taste with salt and black pepper.

To finish

This may sound a little odd, but I like to plate this dish like a Neapolitan ice cream. With that in mind, scoop the stracciatella onto one side each of two serving bowls. Next, scoop the braised cime di rapa into the middle of the bowl, followed by the pesto on the opposing side. It doesn't resemble the Italian flag in any way but still screams Italian to me. Serve with crostini on the side.

AUTUMN

ON SUNDAYS

Grilled English spinach, green olive and oregano

Spinach is one of the best examples of a food that has had its original appeal commodified right out of it. It's become a tasteless green filler. But proper outdoor-grown English spinach has so much flavour and texture. This is one of my favourite dishes because it takes something so underrated, and by adding a few high notes, shows how flavourful and satisfying it can be.

Green olive and oregano pesto

75 g (2¾ oz) green olives, pitted and roughly chopped

20 g (¾ oz) cornichons, roughly chopped

3 g (⅒ oz) capers, roughly chopped

10 g (¼ oz) parmesan, grated

½ shallot, finely diced

1 garlic clove, finely diced

20 g (¾ oz) fresh oregano leaves, roughly chopped

10 g (¼ oz) parsley leaves, roughly chopped

75 g (2¾ oz) olive oil

10 g (¼ oz) lemon juice

To finish

300 g (10½ oz) English spinach, leaves only

vegetable oil

Green olive and oregano pesto

Combine all the ingredients except the olive oil and lemon juice in a bowl and mix well. Pour in the olive oil, give it a good mix and season to taste with salt, black pepper and lemon juice.

To finish

Light a medium-sized fire and let it burn down to a point where it isn't all yellow flames and has a good bed of hot coals, around 45 minutes. Fill a sink with cold water and wash the spinach gently but thoroughly, then drain and spin in a salad spinner to remove any excess water. Working in two batches, place half the spinach into a suitably sized plastic container, then liberally pour in some veg' oil, season well with salt and close the lid. Place a grill tamis sieve onto the fire and give the container a solid shake. This will completely coat each leaf with oil. If you try to grill an un-oiled green leaf it will end up tasting like petrol. Tip the spinach into the tamis sieve and grill over a high heat until softened down, around 30–45 seconds. Make sure you constantly stir the leaves so that they cook evenly and don't scorch. Scoop the olive pesto onto two serving plates and arrange the grilled spinach on top.

Braised escarole, garlic and Espelette bucatini

Cooked bitter-leaf vegetables have so much flavour. The richness and bitterness that's unleashed, especially when punched up with a few well-placed herbs and a bit of spice, makes you wonder why we don't cook more of our salad staples (looking at you, iceberg lettuce). Escarole is often mistaken (or mis-labelled) as endive, perhaps because they're both from the chicory family or perhaps because Australians tend only to have a vague understanding of this vegetable family at the best of times.

Bucatini pasta

300 g (10½ oz) 00 flour
2 g (¹⁄₁₆ oz) salt
semolina, for dusting

To finish

½ head escarole
20 g (¾ oz) olive oil
1 garlic clove, peeled
pinch of Espelette chilli flakes
2 bay leaves
100 g (3½ oz) Fermented fennel juice
    (see page 225)
30 g (1 oz) butter
10 g (¼ oz) fennel leaves, chopped
lemon juice, to taste

Bucatini pasta

Place the flour and salt into the mixer bowl of a pasta extruder machine and turn it on. Slowly add 110 g (4 oz) water while it mixes. Let the dough come together, which should take 2–3 minutes. Flip the machine over to extrude and cut the noodles to around 10 cm (4 in) long, then lightly sprinkle with semolina and lay on a tray.

If you don't have a pasta extruder either try to find someone who sells fresh bucatini or buy a good-quality dried one from an Italian grocery store.

To finish

This dish is best cooked using a wood-fired oven, but if you don't have access to one you could use a rippingly hot gas pizza oven, or a fan-forced oven turned right up as hot it can go. Bring a pot of salted water to the boil to cook the bucatini. Wash the escarole thoroughly in cold water. Cut the root away then chop the leaves through once or twice, then spin dry. Place a large cast-iron pan into a 450°C (842°F) oven. When it is hot, remove and add the olive oil, escarole, garlic, chilli and bay leaves. Season with a little salt and pour in half the fermented fennel juice. Put the pan back in the oven and cook until the leaves soften down (you will need to stir this a few times while it cooks, or the leaves will scorch). Around this time, place the bucatini into the boiling water to cook for around 3 minutes. Once the leaves have wilted down, add the remaining fennel juice and butter to the pan and cook until the liquid reduces to a coating consistency. Remove the pan from the oven one last time and add the drained bucatini and a little pasta water. Add the chopped fennel leaves and season to taste with salt, lemon juice and black pepper.

Raw quince ice cream, honeycomb and nashi pear

I love quince so much I even make booze out of it. If you smell a quince when it's raw, you get an incredible floral complexity. Sadly, to eat that same quince, you have to cook it for a long time, which means you lose its gorgeous aroma. This ice cream is infused with slices of raw quince, ensuring you get that fragrant brightness you'd otherwise miss out on. The quince syrup needs to mature for about 6 months, at best, so you almost need to get ready for this dish a season ahead (remember what I said about how much I love quince).

Raw quince ice cream

400 g (14 oz) milk
100 g (3½ oz) cream
20 g (¾ oz) glucose
20 g (¾ oz) milk powder
95 g (3¼ oz) sugar
1 quince

Quince syrup

1 kg (2 lb 3 oz) quinces
1 kg (2 lb 3 oz) sugar
juice of 2 lemons

Honeycomb

200 g (7 oz) sugar
130 g (4½ oz) glucose
35 g (1¼ oz) honey
10 g (¼ oz) bicarbonate
    of soda (baking soda)

Raw quince ice cream

Place all of the ingredients, except the quince, into a pot and warm over a low heat until everything dissolves. Remove from the heat and chill. Once fully cold, take a sharp knife and finely slice the quince. Add this to the ice cream base. Cover and leave to macerate overnight in the fridge. The following day, strain the mix and process in an ice-cream machine according to the manufacturer's instructions.

Quince syrup

Using a sharp knife, roughly slice the raw quinces and place them in a mixing bowl. Add the sugar and lemon juice. Toss well and transfer everything to a suitably sized glass jar with a tight-fitting lid. Place the jar in the back of your fridge and forget about it for 6 months. Yes, this is a long time, but it is worth it! What will happen over time is that the sugar will draw out the moisture in the quince and then it will slowly ferment into a bright, sparkly quince syrup that tastes like the best parts of a raw quince.

Honeycomb

Find a suitably sized pot to cook this in, keeping in mind that it will expand considerably once the bicarb is added. Find a flat, clean bench and lightly spray it with cooking oil. Next, cover an area about 1 metre (3.2 feet) in length with baking paper. Smooth it down with your hands so that it sticks to the oil coating.

Place the sugar, glucose, honey and 35 g (1¼ oz) water in your pot and heat slowly to ensure the sugar dissolves fully. Once it has, turn the heat up and cook until it reaches 165°C (329°F). The next part is going to happen quickly, so grab a friend to help and a large offset palette knife. Once the honey mix reaches temperature, add the bicarb, give it one good quick stir with a wooden spoon then have your friend slowly pour the boiling, foaming mass along the papered section of benchtop. While this is happening, use the palette knife to spread it out as thinly as possible. Do this as quickly as you can as it will set incredibly fast. (Don't worry, it always works better the second time you make it.) Once it has set, snap it into shards and store in an airtight container.

To finish

Using a sharp knife, cut the pear in half. Cut one half into a small dice and slice the other half finely into thin half-moon shapes. Take four small bowls and add a small pile of the diced nashi to the bottom. Scoop a chunk of ice cream and sit it on top of the nashi. Cover the top of the ice cream with shards of honeycomb and slices of nashi so that they all stand up. Finally, spoon over a little of the fermented quince syrup.

An 'any given
Sunday' Sunday

Is roast chicken the most iconic SUNDAY LUNCH™ you can imagine? A golden, glistening bird coming hot out of the oven on a bed of gnarly veg' – there's a visual appeal here that not many foods can compete with. It hits your memory banks as well as your taste buds. You could even make the argument that any random assortment of people who sit down around a roast chook instantly become a kind of temporary pseudo-family. I'd go along with it, at least until someone snaps the wishbone.

Whenever we have chicken on the menu, we often get asked what makes it so good. In truth, there's no secret. We start with a really good bird, season it properly and pay lots of attention when cooking it. Chicken is interesting because it usually hits the spot even if it's mediocre. But when it's great, you really notice it.

Pushing this menu over the top is a choc ripple tiramisu that is pretty much comfort food on steroids.

Serves 4

(1)   Roast chicken with sauce vin John

(2)   Chloe's salad leaves, house dressing

(3)   Hasselback celeriac, cheddar and peanut

(4)   Choccy ripple-misu (aka 'The Rippa')

Roast chicken
with sauce vin John

Vin Jaune is a classic French wine that's oxidated and aged – almost sherry-like – and so strong that it's quite hard to drink a lot of on its own. But with a little cream, butter and a few aromats, it becomes a legendary sauce for serving with chicken. Sadly, Vin Jaune is also rippingly expensive, so we broke down its flavour profile and gave it a more approachable name.

1 × 1.6 kg (3½ lb) chicken
50 g (1¾ oz) sherry
10 g (¼ oz) roasted garlic
10 g (¼ oz) Dijon mustard
1 g (1/32 oz) fenugreek seeds soaked
    in 20 g (¾ oz) water overnight
100 g (3½ oz) chicken stock
20 g (¾ oz) butter

Place the chicken on a cutting board, breast side up. Using a sharp knife trim the wings off at the joint and remove the wishbone. Halve the chicken by cutting lengthways between the breasts and down over the ribcage. Lay the half flat, skin side down, and remove the bone on the leg. Repeat with the other half. Reserve all trim to make stock on another day. When you are ready to cook, preheat a wood-fired oven to 450°C (842°F). Failing that, a gas pizza oven or convection oven at 220°C (430°F) will work. Heat a cast-iron pan big enough to fit the half-chicken. Lightly oil the pan and season the chicken's skin with salt. Sear, skin side down, over a medium heat for 5 minutes, or until it is starting to get golden brown. Place the pan into the oven and cook for around 14 minutes. Remove the pan and flip the chicken over so that it is skin side up and leave in a warm spot to finish cooking through, around 5–8 minutes. When you are ready to serve, give the chicken a flash through the hot oven for 5 minutes, remove and transfer to a serving plate. Make the sauce in the same pan by putting it over a medium heat and deglazing with the sherry. Once the alcohol has cooked off, add the garlic, mustard, fenugreek (including the soaking water), the stock and butter. Bring everything to a simmer and reduce to a light coating consistency, then season with salt. Finally, spoon the glaze over the chicken and serve.

AUTUMN

ON SUNDAYS

Chloe's salad leaves, house dressing

Never underestimate the impact of a well-thought-out salad. Good ones balance flavour, texture, colour and crunch to create a mix that has body and bite. Chloe, one of our long-term suppliers, is a master at this, which is why this salad has her name on it. Our dressing here is the same one we use at Embla. It's simple and bright – all you need when the leaves are this beautiful.

Embla house dressing
70 g (2½ oz) shallots
20 g (¾ oz) sherry vinegar
140 g (5 oz) olive brine
30 g (1 oz) lemon juice
2 teaspoons mustard powder
5 g (⅛ oz) sugar
50 g (1¾ oz) tamari
150 g (5½ oz) vegetable oil

To finish
200 g (7 oz) fresh salad leaves

Embla house dressing

Place everything, except the oil, into a high-sided jug and blend until smooth using a hand-held blender. Slowly pour in the oil so that it forms an emulsion. Check the seasoning and chill until ready to serve.

To finish

Place the leaves into a mixing bowl, season very lightly with salt and black pepper, and dress lightly with the dressing.

Hasselback celeriac, cheddar and peanut

It's funny how much of cooking is about elevating childhood memories of the food your mum used to make. Here, we take a hasselback potato, which everyone loves, and sub in celeriac – which is a thing people seem to appreciate but don't really cook at home. Pyengana cheddar, made in Tasmania, is, in my opinion, the best cheese that comes out of Australia. Turning it into a sauce is possibly controversial.

ON SUNDAYS

Hasselback celeriac

2 medium celeriacs
4 garlic cloves, very finely sliced
300 g (10½ oz) unsalted butter
60 g (2 oz) rice koji
10 g (¼ oz) thyme, leaves only
1 lemon

Pyengana cheddar sauce

250 g (9 oz) Pyengana cheddar
250 g (9 oz) whey from making
    ricotta (see page 32)
1 garlic clove, peeled

Peanut pesto

75 g (2¾ oz) peanuts, skin on
½ garlic clove, peeled
10 g (¼ oz) parmesan
100 g (3½ oz) peanut oil
5 g (⅛ oz) thyme, leaves only
10 g (14 oz) stout or sherry vinegar

To finish

20 g (¾ oz) butter

Hasselback celeriac

Preheat your oven to 180°C (350°F). Using a sharp knife, trim the outer skin from each celeriac, then cut in half. Using a meat slicer or mandolin, slice the celeriac halves crossways 1.5 mm (¹⁄₁₆ in) thick. You should have thin semi-circles. Save the unsliced ends for later. Put all the cut celeriac into a bowl. Put the garlic into a small pot with the butter and warm over a low heat until the butter is liquid. Pour the butter mix onto the celeriac and add the koji and thyme. Using a microplane, grate in the lemon zest and season well with salt and black pepper. Toss everything so that the marinade is evenly mixed through. Find a high-sided roasting tin and line the bottom of it with baking paper. Now here's the fun part: working slice by slice, stack the celeriac so that it all sits in the same direction, i.e. flat side down and semi-circular side up. Arrange these stacks into rows that are supported by the sides of the baking tray, if your row doesn't make it to the end use the end of the celeriac you saved to hold it up. Cover the tray with aluminium foil and bake for around 1½ hours, or until tender when tested with a skewer. Remove the tray and the foil and chill for at least 1 hour so that the form sets.

Pyengana cheddar sauce

Grate the cheddar using a box grater and combine with the whey and garlic in a small pot. Warm over a low heat so that the cheese doesn't scorch and cook for around 30 minutes. You do not want this to simmer at all, just keep a low even heat so that the flavour and fat separate from the cheese curds, which will seize into a solid mass. Once you have enough flavour, strain off the liquid, discarding the cheese solids and garlic, and season to taste with salt.

Peanut pesto

Using a sharp knife, chop the peanuts through then transfer to a small mixing bowl. Grate the garlic clove and then the parmesan into the bowl using a microplane. Add the oil and thyme, and season well with salt and black pepper. Give it a good mix. Adjust the seasoning with a little of the stout or vinegar.

To finish

Preheat your oven to 450°C (842°F) and place your set hasselback in a cast-iron pan. Put this into the oven to heat through. Test the inside is hot by inserting a cake-testing pin into the middle then holding it against the back of your hand. When it is hot inside, add the butter to the pan, return to the oven, and spoon the melted butter over the hasselback until nicely caramelised. Remove and transfer to a serving dish. Spoon some of the peanut pesto over the top, followed by some of the cheddar sauce.

ON SUNDAYS

Choccy ripple-misu (aka 'The Rippa')

Further to the above, this dessert is our mash-up of a classic tiramisu and the much-loved Australian choccy ripple cake. It's bogan meets Italy, kind of like driving through Portofino in a VL Commodore, with just as much impact. We'll be making all the components, from the biscuits to the coffee and cream. Get this into the fridge the day before so it has time to do its thing.

Chocolate biscuit

150 g (5½ oz) unsalted butter, softened

300 g (10½ oz) sugar

1 egg

200 g (7 oz) plain (all-purpose) flour

80 g (2¾ oz) cocoa

20 g (¾ oz) instant freeze dried coffee powder

1 teaspoon bicarbonate of soda (baking soda)

¼ teaspoon baking powder

½ teaspoon salt

Marsala caramel

250 g (9 oz) Marsala, plus 25 g (1 oz) extra

200 g (7 oz) sugar

900 g (2 lb) espresso, plus 25 g (1 oz) extra

Chocolate biscuit

Preheat a fan-forced oven to 160°C (320°F). Add the butter and sugar to the bowl of a stand mixer fitted with a paddle attachment and whip until the mix has a creamy consistency. Add the egg and beat until combined. Sieve all of the dry ingredients and add to the mixer bowl, then slowly beat until fully combined. At this point you will need to decide what container you are going to build this in. Divide the dough into four, then roll each piece out to the same size and shape of the final serving dish. The dough needs to be 4 mm (¼ in) thick when uncooked. Bake the biscuits on a baking tray lined with baking paper for 6 minutes, then remove to cool.

Marsala caramel

Place the first three ingredients in a small pot and stir over a low heat to dissolve the sugar. Bring to the boil and skim well. Cook over a medium heat until it has reduced down to a thick caramel consistency, then freshen with the second measures of Marsala and coffee. Chill.

Continued next page →

Mascarpone mousse

5 egg yolks

5 g (⅛ oz) gelatine

200 g (7 oz) sugar

50 g (1¾ oz) Marsala

Egg whites

5 egg whites

90 g (3 oz) sugar

Cream

300 g (10½ oz) cream

600 g (1 lb 5 oz) mascarpone

50 g (1¾ oz) Marsala

To finish

cocoa powder, for dusting

Mascarpone mousse

Place the yolks in the bowl of a stand mixer fitted with a whisk attachment. Place the gelatine sheet in a small metal bowl and cover with cold water. Leave to bloom for 5 minutes, then drain off the water. Place the sugar and 100 g (3½ oz) water in a small pot and warm over a low heat until the sugar dissolves. Turn the mixer to high speed and turn the heat up on the pot. Cook the sugar to 117°C (243°F), then slowly pour into the mixer while it is running. Once you have all the sugar in there, knock the speed back to medium. Put the bowl of gelatine over a low flame until it dissolves, then slowly pour into the yolk mix with the Marsala. Turn to low while you make the rest.

For the egg whites, whip the whites to soft peaks while slowly adding the sugar using a stand mixer fitted with a whisk attachment, or by hand.

To make the cream, add everything to a bowl and whip to soft peaks. When you have prepared all the elements, very gently fold the mascarpone into the yolk mix, then finally the whites into the rest. Season with more Marsala if needed.

To finish

Grab your final dish. Working in layers, start with a layer of mousse, then drizzle (for lack of a better word) the caramel over, then add the biscuit. Repeat until you finish with a layer of the mousse, then chill for a minimum of 4 hours so that the mousse sets and the biscuits hydrate slightly. When you're ready to serve, dust with some good-quality cocoa.

AUTUMN

A 'Sunday dread' Sunday

I rarely get Sunday dread these days, which seems strange given my knack for biting off more than I can chew. But I used to get it (mostly on Tuesdays – I had Mondays off), so I know how gut wrenching it can be. Such a shame too, to spend your last few free hours already worrying about the working week ahead.

For me, being around people always helped. So did not being super hungover. But the best way to fully beat the dread was to cook something really damn tasty. After all, you've got to make hay while the sun shines, and sometimes the hay is the happiness you get from great food and conversation. This menu should help get you through Sunday and far enough into Monday that you'll remember that things are rarely as bad as they seem.

Serves 4

(1)   Beef carpaccio, globe artichoke, fermented peppers

(2)   Arrow squid, fennel, ginger and green olive

(3)   Lamb leg, purple-sprouting broccoli, navy beans, anchovy

(4)   Barley koji crème caramel, stout and burnt pear

Beef carpaccio, globe artichoke, fermented peppers

This time of year is when fresh capsicums (bell peppers) are starting to vanish, but they're still really good. At the same time, globe artichokes are just beginning to kick in. This dish celebrates both of these things – particularly the globes, which might actually be my favourite vegetable. You get the puree, which balances the artichoke with a little lemon and fat, then the shavings poached in a light pickle, the ultra-tender slices of beef, and, finally, a red pepper condiment that's so incredibly flavoursome and deep.

ON SUNDAYS

Beef rump

200 g (7 oz) beef rump

Smoked pepper powder

2 red capsicums (bell peppers)

Red pepper condiment

100 g (3½ oz) red capsicums
    (bell peppers)
50 g (1¾ oz) red onion
1 garlic clove, peeled
150 g (5½ oz) vegetable oil
6 g (⅛ oz) Korean chilli
    powder (gochugaru)
30 g (1 oz) Fermented red pepper
    paste (see page 117)
250 g (9 oz) Fermented tomato
    juice (page 225)
50 g (1¾ oz) olive oil

Globe artichoke cream

8 baby globe artichokes
juice of 1 lemon, plus extra
    lemon juice to taste
1 bay leaf
1 garlic clove, halved
75 g (2¾ oz) unsalted butter, diced

Poached globe artichokes

70 g (2½ oz) champagne vinegar
210 g (7½ oz) olive oil
2 garlic cloves
3 sprigs thyme
1 bay leaf
6 baby globe artichokes

Beef rump

Using a sharp knife, trim any sinew or connective tissue from the rump, trying to keep it in as large a piece as possible. Wrap the rump in a layer of biodegradable plastic wrap and freeze for 1½ hours. Once it has firmed right up, unwrap it and use a meat slicer to shave into 1 mm (¹⁄₁₆ in) thick slices. Lay these slices onto a piece of baking paper in a single layer, then chill.

Smoked pepper powder

Using a sharp knife, cut the peppers in half lengthways and remove the seeds. Grill each half over a hot fire quickly – enough to give it a good char – then place on a rack high above the fire to dry overnight. Once dry, grind into a fine powder.

Red pepper condiment

Using a sharp knife, cut the red capsicum and red onion into small 4 mm (¼ in)-ish dice. Slice the garlic clove as finely as possible. Put all of the ingredients, except the veg' oil, into a small pot, season with salt and add 30 g (1 oz) of the oil. Sweat over a low heat until it all just begins to soften, then add the rest of the ingredients, making sure that the pepper paste is mixed in evenly. Cook over a low heat until it comes together, around 15 minutes. Remove and let it cool, then season well with salt.

Globe artichoke cream

Using a sharp knife, peel off the outer hard green leaves from the artichokes, cut them in half and place in a small pot. Pour in enough water to just cover, then squeeze in the juice of 1 lemon. Add the bay and garlic. Season with salt and bring to the boil, then simmer gently until the artichokes are soft. Drain off the artichokes, making sure to reserve the liquid. Put them in an upright blender and blend until smooth. Add chunks of cold butter and a little water if needed to create a thick, smooth puree. Season this to taste with salt and lemon juice. Pass through a fine sieve and chill.

Poached globe artichokes

Find a small pot and place all the ingredients in, except for the artichokes. Using your hands, remove all the tough exterior leaves and then use a sharp knife to trim away any remaining tough green exterior. Grab a mandolin and very carefully shave the artichokes 2 mm (¹⁄₁₆ in) thick, then submerge the slices into the pickle mix. Season well with salt and warm gently over a medium heat. They will not need a lot of cooking so watch it and remove as soon as they begin to wilt. Chill in the pickle brine to stop the cooking process.

To finish

Grab two serving dishes and scoop four small spoons of the artichoke cream into the middle of each plate. On top of these dollops, place slices of the drained poached artichoke. Next, lay over the slices of beef in a single layer. Season the beef with salt and black pepper then spoon over a little of the red pepper condiment. Finally, dust with the smoked pepper powder.

Arrow squid, fennel, ginger and green olive

Australia's go-to cephalopod is calamari – by quite a large margin. But I think the humble squid is meatier and a lot less sweet. It's a shame squid isn't used more often because it really is suitable for a lot more preparations. To avoid turning your kitchen into an inky mess, get a fishmonger to clean the hood for you. Once you get it home, the secret is cooking it hard and fast before slicing it nice and thin.

Squid
1 large arrow squid

Ginger pil pil
trim from the squid prep (see above)
1 fennel bulb
3 garlic cloves
2 shallots
2 bay leaves
½ rosemary sprig
100 g (3½ oz) green olives
100 g (3½ oz) ginger, peeled
    and sliced
Fish skin stock (page 225)
100 g (3½ oz) olive oil
vegetable oil
lemon juice, to taste

Fennel
2 fennel bulbs
vegetable oil

To finish
10 green Sicilian olives
10 g (¼ oz) Fermented fennel
    seeds (see page 225)
vegetable oil
lemon juice, to taste
50 g (1¾ oz) chickweed
50 g (1¾ oz) wild watercress

Squid

Clean the squid by first separating the hood and the tentacles using your hands. Remove the beak and anything else that remains inside, and peel away the thin outer skin also. Lay the hood on a chopping board and use a sharp knife to cut the hood in half along the natural seam. Turn each half so that the inside is facing upwards and score in a fine crosshatch pattern, making sure to not cut all the way through. Trim the portion into shape if needed, cut the stomach away from the tentacles and reserve any trim.

Ginger pil pil

Place all the ingredients, except the oils and lemon juice, into a suitably sized pot and pour in enough fish stock to cover. Bring to the boil and give it a couple of skims to remove any foam that arises. Add the olive oil, turn down to a simmer and cook gently for 30 minutes, or until the stock has reduced slightly and it is full of flavour. Remove from the heat, ladle gently through a fine sieve and leave to cool to room temperature. Once cooled, put the stock in an upright blender and turn to high speed. Very slowly pour in cold vegetable oil so that the protein in the stock forms an emulsion with the oil. You will need to eyeball this and taste as you go along. Once it is to your liking, turn it off and season with salt and lemon juice.

Fennel

Preheat your wood-fired oven to 450°C (842°F). Using a sharp knife, cut the fennel bulbs into quarters vertically, so that the root still holds the layers together. Lightly oil and season with salt, then place in a cast-iron pan and roast in the wood oven until just softened. Remove and leave to cool enough to handle, then slice finely.

To finish

Light a fire and let it cook down, or get your barbecue nice and hot. Place the roasted fennel, olives and fennel seeds in a heat-proof bowl and leave in a reasonably warm spot while you cook the squid. Warm a little of the ginger pil pil in a small pot. Lightly oil the squid and season with salt. Grill over the hot coals, scored side down, until it curls up into a tube. This should take roughly a minute and you should be able to see the squid's colour turn from opaque to white. Remove from the fire and slice as finely as you can, then add to the fennel bowl. Spoon in a little of the pil pil, some lemon juice and season with salt. Give it an even mix then add the leaves and give it a very gentle toss through before transferring to a serving bowl.

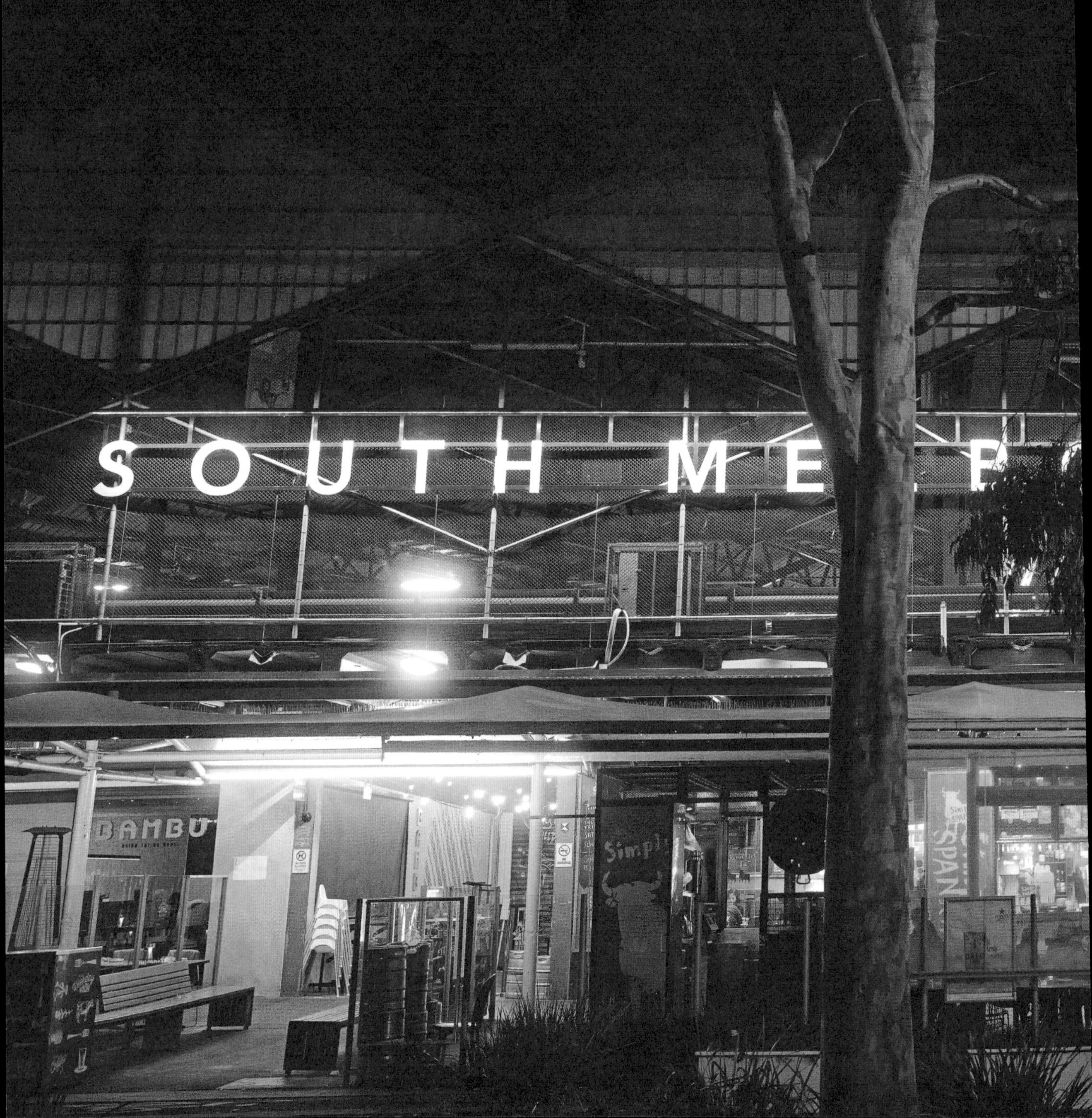
SOUTH ME
BAMBU
Simply

ON SUNDAYS

Lamb leg, purple-sprouting broccoli, navy beans, anchovy

There's nothing overtly fishy going on here, just a few anchovies adding some rich savoury notes that go great with the meaty richness of the lamb fat. It's a classic pairing, just so long as you don't use the same anchovies you used to get on those 1980s marinara pizzas. The navy beans carry everything along nicely, while also bringing a satisfying little pop.

Lamb leg

1 × 1 kg (2 lb 3 oz) boneless lamb leg
50 g (1¾ oz) oregano
5 garlic cloves
1 bay leaf
1 shallot
5 g (⅛ oz) rosemary leaves
5 g (⅛ oz) salt
20 g (¾ oz) rice koji
100 g (3½ oz) olive oil
zest of ½ lemon

Navy beans

100 g (3½ oz) dried navy beans, soaked overnight
2 garlic cloves, peeled
1 bay leaf

Macadamia pesto

50 g (1¾ oz) macadamia nuts
1 g (¹⁄₃₂ oz) thyme, leaves only
½ garlic clove, peeled
zest of ½ lemon
20 g (¾ oz) lemon juice
20 g (¾ oz) parsley, leaves only
15 g (½ oz) capers
10 g (¼ oz) oregano
70 g (2½ oz) vegetable oil
25 g (1 oz) olive oil

To finish

150 g (5½ oz) purple-sprouting broccoli
vegetable oil
150 g (5½ oz) lamb stock
2 anchovies, chopped
20 g (¾ oz) olive oil

Lamb leg

You will need to start this the night before you would like to cook the lamb. Using a sharp knife, butterfly the lamb leg open and place into a non-reactive container. Make a marinade by blending the rest of the ingredients together using a hand-held blender. Pour this onto the lamb, making sure to cover all of the leg. Cover and chill overnight. The next day, light a good fire and let it burn down to a solid bed of coals. Using your hands, remove most of the marinade and place the lamb onto a rack around 1 metre (3.2 feet) above the surface of the fire. Cook slowly for around 1¼ hours, or until it reaches 50°C (122°F) when tested with a thermometer. The trick here is to manage the heat so that it is consistent but slow; the slower the cook the more tender it will be. Remove from the fire and let it rest, covered, in a warm spot for 10 minutes.

Navy beans

Drain the beans, put in a small pot and cover with water. Bring to the boil and give it a couple of good skims to remove any foam. Turn the heat down to just below a simmer and add the aromats. Cook very gently for 1½ hours, or until just tender and creamy. Remove the pot from the heat and cool as quickly as possible while keeping the beans submerged.

Macadamia pesto

Place everything, except the oils, into the bowl of a small blender and pulse until roughly chopped. Add in both oils and pulse once to combine. Check the seasoning and season with salt if need be.

To finish

Preheat a wood-fired oven to 450°C (842°F). Oil the sprouting broccoli with the vegetable oil and season with salt. Place in a cast-iron pan and cook in the oven until the broccoli starts to get soft. Add the lamb stock, navy beans and anchovy and continue cooking until everything has warmed through. Remove from the oven, check the seasoning and add the olive oil. Carve the lamb leg and transfer to a serving dish then top with the sprouting broccoli. Spoon some of the pesto on the side and finish with the navy beans and sauce.

Barley koji crème caramel, stout and burnt pear

Something I love to do is present a thing that is unfamiliar in a reassuringly familiar form. This take on a classic dessert is a good example. You get the crème caramel you know and love, but it comes with this incredible roasted barley koji flavour, which is fragrant and almost chicory-like. Combatting the sweetness is a caramel deglazed with stout and pears poached in verjuice. You will need to start the custard a day ahead.

Custard

60 g (2 oz) barley koji
150 g (5½ oz) milk
400 g (14 oz) cream
45 g (1½ oz) egg yolks
65 g (2¼ oz) sugar

Stout caramel

200 g (7 oz) sugar
100 g (3½ oz) stout beer

Burnt pear

150 g (5½ oz) sugar
250 g (9 oz) white verjuice
½ vanilla bean
1 bay leaf
3 beurre bosc pears
stout vinegar or sherry vinegar, to season

Custard

Preheat the oven to 180°C (350°F) and place the barley koji on a baking tray. Bake the koji until light golden brown, around 8 minutes, then leave to cool. Put the milk and cream in a small pot and bring to 60°C (140°F) over a low heat. Pour into a plastic container and add the barley. Leave to cool to room temperature. Put the yolks and sugar in a small bowl and, using a whisk, quickly beat together. Add the yolk mix into the milk infusion and whisk lightly to combine, then cover and refrigerate overnight. The following day, preheat the oven to 140°C (285°F) and find a high-sided baking tray deep enough to hold your chosen ramekins. Strain off the custard mix through a fine strainer, making sure to not create too many bubbles or aerate in any way. Pour 125 g (4½ oz) of the custard mix into each of the four ramekins. Fold a tea towel (dish towel) and place it into the bottom of your baking tray, then place the ramekins on top. Fill the tray with hot tap water to just below the level of the custard. Cover the tray with foil and carefully transfer it to the oven. Bake for around 40 minutes or until the custards wobble as one even mass. Remove the custards from the tray and leave to cool at room temperature, then chill to set.

Stout caramel

Put the sugar and 80 g (2¾ oz) water in a small pot set over a low heat and warm until the sugar dissolves. Once it has, turn the heat up and cook until you reach a medium dark caramel. Take the pot off the heat and leave to the side while the caramel continues to darken. Once it has gotten to a deep, rich colour very carefully add the stout and swirl until evenly combined.

Burnt pear

Preheat a wood-fired oven to 450°C (842°F). Put the sugar, 300 g (10½ oz) water, vanilla and bay leaf in a small pot. Peel the pears, cut in half, trim off the stem and remove the core. Put into the pot and poach over a medium heat until slightly overcooked. Remove the pears from the liquid and transfer to a cast-iron pan. Roast the poached pears in the oven until well charred on all sides, then remove and leave to cool. Once cool enough to handle use a knife to chop them through until you have a textural paste. Season with stout vinegar.

To serve

Remove each custard from the fridge and spoon on enough stout caramel to cover the top of each. Take the burnt pear compote and, using two spoons, carefully shape a quenelle and place on top of each.

AUTUMN

A Sunday with strangers

This menu was originally titled 'A Sunday meeting your long-time-single best friend's brand new romantic partner' but it seemed too weird and specific. The basic idea though, which we've decided to keep, is that not all Sunday lunches happen between old mates with lots to talk about. Sometimes a little conversation insurance – interesting quirks and talking points hidden in and around the meal – can be handy.

So here we have a menu of dishes that can hopefully get you unstuck if the chat dries up. And, failing that, everything should still taste pretty good eaten in silence.

Serves 4

(1)   Tuna carpaccio, capers, fermented buttermilk ricotta

(2)   Pork rillettes, shallots, sprouts and crisp sage

(3)   Octopus, borlotti beans, turnip and walnut

(4)   Hemp seed pavlova, lime, fennel and green apple

Tuna carpaccio, capers, fermented buttermilk ricotta

This dish reminds me of the cottage cheese I grew up eating. It's also a bit of a mainstay at Embla, where we ferment the buttermilk in-house before setting it into a gorgeous and mildly acidic ricotta. The thinly sliced and flattened tuna gives you a delicate mouthfeel while the capers add brightness and bite.

Buttermilk ricotta mix

100 g (3½ oz) home-made ricotta
  (see page 32)
60 g (2 oz) cultured buttermilk
10 g (¼ oz) olive oil
25 g (1 oz) baby capers,
  roughly chopped
5 g (⅛ oz) chives, finely chopped
1 g (1/32 oz) tarragon, finely chopped
½ teaspoon finely diced shallot
zest of ¼ lemon

Tuna carpaccio

5 g (⅛ oz) vegetable oil
150 g (5½ oz) line-caught tuna

To serve

olive oil, for drizzling

Buttermilk ricotta mix

Grab a small mixing bowl and add the ricotta, buttermilk and olive oil. Add the capers, herbs and shallot, and microplane in the lemon zest, then give it a good mix. Season to taste with salt and black pepper.

Tuna carpaccio

You will need to serve this dish on very flat plates, so find the ones you'll use and cut four squares of baking paper the same size as the plate. Using a pastry brush, lightly brush one side of each piece of paper with the oil. Cut the tuna in half and sandwich each slice with the oiled paper. Using a meat mallet gently but firmly bash out the tuna flat. You will need it to spread to the size of the flat area of your plate. Once you've spread it that far give it a quick roll over with a rolling pin to smooth it nicely. Chill to set.

To serve

Take your serving plates and scoop a good spoonful of the buttermilk ricotta mix onto each one. Using the back of your spoon spread it out to the same size as the tuna. Carefully peel away one of the sides of paper from the tuna and lay the tuna on top of the buttermilk. Gently press down and then remove the top layer of paper. Season with a little salt and lightly drizzle on some olive oil.

AUTUMN

Pork rillettes, shallots, sprouts and crisp sage

This is a classic pork rillettes with a few added touches to lighten and balance everything out. Traditional rillettes have a way of feeling a bit pasty, due to overly shredded, slow-cooked meat. In this version we don't shred, which means you get a more varied texture. Shallots give roasty vegetal notes while the mung bean sprouts (sprout them at home!) are almost like fresh peanuts – so tasty. The sage is there because pork obviously loves sage. Start sprouting the mung beans few days ahead of serving.

Mung bean sprouts

50 g (1¾ oz) dried mung beans

Rillettes

400 g (14 oz) skinless pork belly

400 g (14 oz) pork shoulder

100 g (3½ oz) shallots, peeled

40 g (1½ oz) garlic cloves, peeled

200 g (7 oz) pork back fat, diced
into 1 cm (½ in) chunks

Shallots

3 banana shallots

30 g (1 oz) olive oil

To finish

20 g (¾ oz) sage

50 g (1¾ oz) vegetable oil

20 g (¾ oz) olive oil

grilled sourdough, to serve

Mung bean sprouts

Cover the mung beans with cold water and soak for 8 hours, being sure to remove any beans that float or any other impurities that turn up. Take a glass jar and add the soaked mung beans, cover the opening with a small piece of muslin (cheesecloth) and fix into place with a rubber band. Under a tap run water into the jar until the beans are covered, then drain off the water again. You are going to repeat this same wetting action four times a day until they are fully sprouted. Once drained, put the jar in a warm spot but not in direct sunlight. The idea here is to germinate the bean, so you want to keep it moist but not wet. Mung beans are quick, and they should be good to go in about 36 hours.

Rillettes

Light a fire just before you start prepping the pork. Using a sharp knife cut both the pork belly and the pork shoulder into 2.5 cm (1 in) cubes. Lightly oil and season the pork belly then spread in an even layer on a rack. Place the rack high above your fire and slowly smoke for 1½ hours. During this time the belly will cook a little and that's fine, what you don't want is for the heat to be too high and for the belly to cook too hard and tighten up. Preheat the oven to 170°C (340°F). Once the belly is smelling delicious and has taken on a nice amount of smoke, transfer it to a braising dish, add the remaining ingredients and a small dash of water. Cover with a tight-fitting lid and braise in the oven until soft to the touch, around 2½ hours. Remove from the oven and leave until cool enough to handle. Using your hands, shred the pork down and emulsify the fat with any moisture that has come from the meat. Season to taste with salt.

Shallots

Using a sharp knife, peel the shallots and split them in half lengthways. Take a cast-iron pan and add the olive oil. Place the shallots in the pan, cut side down, and season with salt. Put the pan above the fire and slowly cook until caramelised and soft, around 1 hour. Let them cool then roughly chop.

To finish

Take a small pan and fry the sage in the vegetable oil until crisp. Remove from the pan and season with salt. Take a third of the pork rillettes mix and put it into a small bowl. The remainder of the mix will keep in the fridge. Add the caramelised shallots, olive oil, sage and a handful of the sprouted mung beans. Give it a mix and check the seasoning, adjusting with salt and black pepper. Finally, give it a good whip and transfer to a serving plate. This goes great with freshly grilled sourdough.

Octopus, borlotti beans, turnip and walnut

Nine times out of ten you marinate your protein before you cook it, but some proteins are hard to get flavour into when they're raw. Large octopus tentacles are a prime example. To make this dish, you're first going to cook the octopus before dunking it into the marinade. As it cools down, it'll draw in more flavour, creating wicked depth. Borlotti beans, turnip and walnuts are there for their savoury notes.

Octopus

2 large octopus tentacles
250 g (9 oz) vegetable oil, plus extra for oiling
150 g (5½ oz) olive oil
100 g (3½ oz) sherry vinegar
20 g (¾ oz) oregano
25 g (1 oz) lemon thyme
5 g (⅛ oz) salt
4 garlic cloves, peeled
1 rosemary sprig

Borlotti beans

500 g (1 lb 2 oz) fresh borlotti beans
2 bay leaves

Confit shallots

2 banana shallots, peeled
4 garlic cloves, peeled
70 g (2½ oz) vegetable oil
40 g (1½ oz) white wine

To finish

1 turnip
150 g (5½ oz) Fish skin stock (page 225)
100 g (3½ oz) walnuts, roughly chopped
10 g (¼ oz) chives, roughly chopped
20 g (¾ oz) unsalted butter
10 g (¼ oz) olive oil

Octopus

Preheat an oven to 160°C (320°F). Lightly oil and season the octopus tentacles and place into a braising dish large enough to hold them. Add in a small splash of water then cover with a tight-fitting lid. Put the dish into the oven and cook for around 1½ hours, or until the octopus is tender when tested with a skewer. While the octopus is cooking make the marinade by placing all the other ingredients into a pot and gently warming up to 50°C (122°F). Remove from the heat and pour the marinade into a container large enough to fit the marinade and the octopus and keep in a warm spot. Once the octopus is cooked, transfer it straight into the warm marinade and leave to cool.

Borlotti beans

Pod the borlotti beans and place them in a small pot. Cover with water and slowly bring to the boil. Give it a good skim to remove any impurities, add the bay leaves and a good pinch of salt. Simmer gently over a medium heat until the beans are just tender, then remove the pan from the heat and leave to cool in the liquid.

Confit shallots

Using a sharp knife, dice both the shallots and garlic as fine as you can, then transfer to a small pot. Add a little of the oil, season with salt and sweat over a low heat for 5 minutes. Turn the heat up and add the wine, let it cook down by half then add the rest of the oil. Cook over a low heat until the shallots are soft and sweet. Remove from the heat when done.

To finish

Light a fire and let it burn down to a solid bed of coals. Using a sharp knife dice the turnip into 5 mm (¼ in) squares. Grab a small pot and add the stock and diced turnip. Cook over a medium heat until the turnip begins to soften. At this point add the borlotti beans and a spoonful of the confit shallot mix, then simmer until warmed through. Finish by stirring through the walnuts, chives, butter and olive oil. Season well with salt and black pepper, then divide between two serving bowls.

Remove the octopus from the marinade and let the oil drain off a little. Grill over a high heat until the outer skin has crisped up and taken on some nice colour. Take off the grill and cut each tentacle lengthways using a knife, then arrange two halves in each bowl.

ON SUNDAYS

Hemp seed pavlova, lime, fennel and green apple

Pavlova isn't known for being a refreshing dessert, but with the inherent lightness of meringue, it doesn't take much to brighten it up. The process of making this shouldn't weigh you down either – all of it can and should be done in advance so that on the day, all you have to do is put it together.

Hemp seed pavlova
100 g (3½ oz) egg whites
0.5 g (⅟₃₂ oz) cream of tartar
110 g (4 oz) sugar
15 g (½ oz) hemp seeds

Lime posset
1 g (⅟₃₂ oz) gelatine sheet
125 g (4½ oz) cream
zest of ½ lime
40 g (1½ oz) sugar
25 g (1 oz) lime juice

Candied fennel
80 g (2¾ oz) sugar
1 strip lemon zest
½ fennel bulb

Green apple sorbet
250 g (9 oz) green apple juice
60 g (2 oz) glucose
30 g (1 oz) sugar
225 g (8 oz) green apple, peeled and diced

To serve
10 g (¼ oz) fennel leaves

Hemp seed pavlova

Preheat the oven to 100°C (212°F) with no fan. Put the whites and cream of tartar into the bowl of a stand mixer fitted with a whisk attachment. Turn to a medium–fast speed and, when the whites begin to foam, slowly start adding the sugar. Once you have incorporated all of the sugar, turn the speed right down and sprinkle in the hemp seeds, lightly mix through and turn off. Transfer the meringue to a piping (pastry) bag. Line a baking tray with baking paper or a silicone mat and place the tray onto a set of scales. Pipe the meringue into 30 g (1 oz) mounds. Using the back of a spoon, gently push a small divot in the top so that you have somewhere to balance the rest of the ingredients when you plate. Place the tray in the oven and cook for 1 hour, then crack the door slightly open and turn the oven off. Leave to cool then store in an airtight container until ready to serve.

Lime posset

Soak the gelatine in cold water for 5 minutes. Once soft, squeeze to remove any excess water. To a small pot add the cream, lime zest and sugar. Bring this mix to the boil, add the softened gelatine and swirl the pot off the heat until it dissolves. Add the lime juice, stir to combine then pass through a fine-mesh sieve into a small container. Chill until set, around 2 hours.

Candied fennel

Put the sugar in a small pot with 120 g (4½ oz) water and add the lemon zest. Take the fennel bulb and, using a knife, cut into 2 mm (⅟₁₆ in) fine dice. Add this to the syrup and simmer gently over a low heat until the fennel slightly loses its rawness, about 3–6 minutes. Chill immediately over an ice bath.

Green apple sorbet

In a small pot set over a medium heat, bring the apple juice, glucose and sugar up to 80°C (176°F). Pour the syrup into a container and chill. Once the syrup is completely cold blend with the fresh apple until smooth. Freeze in an ice-cream machine according to the manufacturer's instructions.

To serve

Put a tiny amount of the lime posset onto your serving plate then place the pavlova on top – this will stop it sliding around. Scoop a more generous spoon of the posset into the divot you made earlier. Drain the candied fennel and spoon on top of the posset. Add some fennel leaves, then finish with a scoop of the apple sorbet.

Mushroom picking

Embla gets its mushrooms from a chef-turned-producer called Matt who's been picking wild pines, slippery jacks, grey ghosts, wood blewits and Australian morels, as well as the odd parasol, for the better part of 15 years. I say *better* part because Matt believes mushroom picking changed his life, affording him a lifestyle and a way of working that's completely different from running his own successful Melbourne restaurant. I can probably guess what he means by that.

Picking mushrooms yourself is one of the great available pastimes. You're out in a forest, breathing clean air, collecting delicious little umami bombs free of charge. Picking is as simple as happening upon one, slicing it off at the stem and covering the patch of ground back up so another mushroom can grow in its place. But there are nuances, which is why I asked Matt for his own set of mushrooming tips. Have funghi!

Matt's mushrooming dos and don'ts

Do   When starting out, stick to picking pine mushrooms and slippery jacks. Both are delicious, plentiful within short drives of metro areas and are difficult to mistake for anything dangerous. Your target size is anything up to the diameter of a cut grapefruit – anything larger can be woody or contain parasites. Slippery jacks are less popular with chefs because you do have to cook a fair bit of water out of them, but I reckon they're worth the extra effort.

Don't   Pull up and start picking right on top of where someone else is picking. Use your judgement and give everyone plenty of space. Chances are you'll be on public land, but even so, a bit of respect goes a long way. Same goes for littering and house music.

Do   Track the weather. Mushrooms are said to be seasonal but it's not like they're looking at a calendar. You can get them anytime the conditions are right and I've even picked a flush of them at Christmas. Once you've identified a mushrooming spot (anywhere with a decent amount of pine trees) use a weather app to keep an eye on rainfall. A good bit of rain and temperatures of around 20°C (68°F) should make for a good haul.

Don't   Get caught up buying expensive gear. There are specific mushroom knives out there, but I favour a regular little serrated Victorinox that does the job just as well. Any basket or box will do too, but bring kitchen paper or tea towels (dish towels) to layer between your mushrooms so that they're not stacked right on top of each other. Other than that, pack a warm jumper and wet weather gear if rain might be on the cards. Picking in the rain makes it hard to keep your mushrooms in good nick though, so try to go when it's dry.

Do   Sleep in. Unlike fishing or hunting, you don't need to be up before the sun. When spotting mushrooms, daylight is your friend. Also unlike fishing and hunting, mushroom picking isn't about battling the elements. It's pretty much walking with benefits.

Don't   Pick more than you can eat. It sounds obvious but by the same token, walking away from mushrooms when they're right there in front of you can be challenging.

Do   Bring a couple of mates and make a day of it. Take a picnic blanket and a little gas stove and cook them up fresh. Can you think of a better day trip than that? Conversely, go by yourself. Let your body go into autopilot and use the time, as I do, to think or catch up on your audiobooks. But however you choose to do it, get out there and enjoy the surroundings.

Pine mushroom barigoule

500 g (1 lb 2 oz) small pine mushrooms

2 garlic cloves, peeled

125 g (4½ oz) champagne vinegar

300 g (10½ oz) olive oil

15 g (½ oz) thyme, leaves only

2 bay leaves

6 g (⅛ oz) salt

Clean the pine mushrooms by wiping away any dirt with a damp cloth. Using a sharp knife, cut them down to an even size. Split the garlic cloves in half, then put everything into a small pot set over a medium heat. Cook gently until the mushrooms begin to soften, then remove from the heat and transfer to a clean container to cool. Keep refrigerated. This is delicious on anything from toast to a quick pasta garnish.

Pine mushrooms, peppers and red rice

Red rice base

20 g (¾ oz) olive oil

30 g (1 oz) unsalted butter

250 g (9 oz) Kerala red rice

250 g (9 oz) Fermented tomato juice (page 225)

125 g (4½ oz) olive brine

65 g (2¼ oz) caper brine

30 g (1 oz) Confit shallots and garlic (see page 160)

15 g (½ oz) Fermented pepper paste (see page 117)

pinch of saffron threads

2 bay leaves

To finish

30 g (1 oz) vegetable oil

500 g (1 lb 2 oz) pine mushrooms, sliced

50 g (1¾ oz) unsalted butter

10 g (¼ oz) rosemary leaves

10 g (¼ oz) sherry vinegar

Red rice base

Preheat your wood-fired oven and light a fire for your grill ahead of time. Place the rice in a bowl and wash under cold running water until the water runs clear, then cover it with water and let it soak for 30 minutes before draining thoroughly. Take a low-sided cast-iron pan or paella pan and warm it over the fire. Add the oil, butter and red rice and sweat over a medium–low heat for 2 minutes. Add all the remaining ingredients, along with 1.25 kg (2 lb 12 oz) water and season with salt. Bring to the boil and simmer without stirring for 20–25 minutes. The trick here is to manage your heat source so that it doesn't scorch in any one spot and that all of the liquid has cooked out by the time the rice is done. Believe me, it's easier the second time you do it!

To finish

Grab a cast-iron pan and heat it in your wood-fired oven. When it's nice and hot add the vegetable oil and mushrooms. Season with salt and roast in the oven under tender, about 6–7 minutes. Near the end of the cooking time, add the butter and rosemary and stir through. When ready, pull the pan out and season with black pepper and the vinegar, then spoon the mushrooms and butter over the rice.

Wild mushrooms, porcini and preserved quince

Dried porcini mushroom butter
200 g (7 oz) unsalted butter
2 g (1/16 oz) salt
18 g (2/3 oz) dried porcini
  mushroom powder
2 garlic cloves, peeled

Salt-preserved quince
2 quinces
salt

Quince vinegar
1 quince
1 kg (2 lb 3 oz) white vinegar

To finish
30 g (1 oz) olive oil
300 g (10½ oz) mixed mushrooms
1 garlic clove, finely sliced

Dried porcini mushroom butter
Using a knife, dice the butter and leave it to soften slightly at room temperature for an hour or so. Transfer it to a bowl blender with the salt and porcini powder. Grab a microplane and grate the garlic in. Blend on high until smooth, then decant into a clean container and chill to set.

Salt-preserved quince
This is a great larder item that allows you to extend quince season. To start, wash the quinces well under cold running water, then use a knife to cut them into quarters. Find yourself a suitably sized container and sprinkle a layer of salt on the bottom. Working one by one, layer in the quince quarters and enough salt to completely cover them. Cover with a lid and leave in a cool spot for 4–6 months. When ready to use, remove them from the salt and wash under cold water. Pat them dry and then use a sharp knife to cut them into fine strips.

Quince vinegar
Use a knife to finely slice the raw quince. Transfer the slices to a vacuum-pack bag and pour in the vinegar. Seal on high pressure then steam at 65°C (149°F) in an oven for 1½ hours, or in a medium sized pot of water at 65°C (149°F) for 1 hour. Remove from the oven to cool. Ideally you would want to let this chill for at least a week to develop.

To finish
Preheat a wood-fired oven to 450°C (842°F). At the restaurant we cook this in a terracotta baking dish, but you could also use a smallish cast-iron pan. Ideally, use something presentable as we'll serve it in the same thing it cooks in. If you're using a terracotta dish make sure to soak it overnight first or it will crack in the heat of the oven. Place your dish into the oven to heat. Oil and season your mushrooms and, when the dish is really hot, tip your mushrooms in and put it back in the wood oven for 6 minutes. About halfway through the cook, add the sliced garlic and a very healthy spoon of the porcini mushroom butter, stir it through quickly and finish the cook. This should take only around 4 minutes. Once cooked, pull the dish out and squirt some of the quince vinegar in to balance the richness. Finally, scatter with the salted quince and serve.

(4)　Winter

A fireside Sunday

Open fires are a bit of a luxury these days, and spending a whole afternoon in front of one is an even rarer thing. They are pretty damn lovely. I could try to go on about all the different ways they're lovely but I'm a chef, not a poet, so I'll leave that for someone better with words. I will say though that things do taste better when you're in close proximity to flame. Wine, for example. Cheese.

Think of this menu as something you can dish out on a lazy weekend away in the country with a partner or a close friend. It's all snacky stuff that can be done ahead of time so you don't have to be away from the fireplace cooking for too long. The exception is the crispbread, which needs to be made then and there for maximum crispness.

Serves 4

(1)   Sardine toasts with lemon and mustard

(2)   Crudites with whipped anchovy and nettles

(3)   Smoked duck liver parfait, new walnuts, old walnuts

(4)   Condiments and things to eat with cheese

Sardine toasts with lemon and mustard

Sardines, with the punchy heat of mustard, cut with the acid brightness of lemon. It's a combo we've done in different variations for years. As with many – but not all – things, spending a little extra to get better-quality sardines will make a noticeable difference. You can even buy fresh ones and preserve them yourself if you're that way inclined. Extra points for those who eat this with self-baked bread (see page 217).

Mustard butter

200 g (7 oz) unsalted butter
60 g (2 oz) Dijon mustard
25 g (1 oz) wholegrain mustard
25 g (1 oz) crème fraîche

To finish

8 slices of focaccia
20 g (¾ oz) olive oil
1 Meyer lemon
8 preserved sardines

Mustard butter

Dice the butter into rough, small chunks using a sharp knife. Transfer to a mixing bowl and leave somewhere warm to soften to room temperature. When soft but not melted, add both mustards and beat until smooth using a spatula. Season with salt until you're happy and then add the crème fraîche. Gently fold through until combined – if you beat this too much it will split.

To finish

Take each slice of focaccia and brush or drizzle some of the olive oil over it. Toast in a wood-fired oven until lightly golden on all sides, around 3 minutes. Remove the toast from the oven and transfer to a tray to cool slightly. Using a very sharp knife or a mandolin, slice the whole lemon as finely as you can. When the toast has cooled enough, spoon a healthy amount of the mustard butter on top, then pop a sardine fillet on top of the butter. Lastly, arrange the lemon slices artfully and serve.

Crudites with whipped anchovy and nettles

Chip and dip for adults. The anchovy here acts the same way that egg yolk does in an aioli – it's the emulsifier bringing everything together. It also packs in heaps of flavour without being overly fishy. The cooked nettles have an iron-y, bright-green wholesomeness, a little like spinach, but bigger. Serve with lots of the freshest veg' available.

Whipped anchovy cream

150 g (5½ oz) sourdough

2 tins of good anchovies (about 100 g/3½ oz in total)

1 garlic clove, peeled

½ shallot, peeled

250 g (9 oz) vegetable oil

40 g (1½ oz) lemon juice

Nettle salsa

250 g (9 oz) picked nettles

1 small shallot, peeled

1 garlic clove, peeled

100 g (3½ oz) capers

50 g (1¾ oz) olive oil

To finish

6 chicory (endive) leaves

6 sorrel leaves

6 spigarello broccoli leaves

2 small fennel bulbs

¼ head of Romanesco

1 yellow witlof (Belgian endive)

4 kipfler (fingerling) potatoes

Whipped anchovy cream

Using a sharp knife, cut away any crust from the sourdough, then cut the centre into large chunks. Cover the bread with cold water and soak for 5 minutes, then use your hands to squeeze out most of the moisture. Drain the oil from the anchovies and place in an upright blender. Add the bread, garlic and shallot. Turn to a medium speed and slowly pour in the vegetable oil to form a smooth emulsion. Once you've added all the oil, stop the blender and scrape down the side of the bowl, check the seasoning and adjust with lemon juice and salt. Blend till smooth.

Nettle salsa

You are going to need to use gloves here; nettles will prick you and it will get itchy! Bring a small pot of water to the boil and prep a bowl full of iced water. Blanch the nettles for 5 seconds, then drain. Tip the nettles into the iced water to stop the cooking process. Blanching them quickly like this will get rid of their ability to sting or cause any itchiness. When they're cold, squeeze out any excess water. Place the shallot and garlic in a small bowl blender and pulse until they're broken down. Add the blanched nettles, capers and olive oil. Pulse this again until everything has come together but still retains some texture. Season to taste with salt and black pepper.

To finish

You really can use any vegetables here, but I have listed some of my favourites that we serve in the restaurant. Wash all of your vegetables individually and, using a knife, break them down into manageable-sized versions. Take the kipfler potatoes and cook them in salted water until tender, then let them cool and cut in half. Arrange the vegetables on a flat serving dish and scoop the anchovy and nettle salsa into a small serving bowl.

Smoked duck liver parfait,
new walnuts,
old walnuts

This is a great platform for your Pickled black walnuts (page 117) and something we've riffed on at Embla quite a bit. The parfait is very rich and fatty – just as it should be – but there's enough texture and acid to keep it under control. At Embla we use beautiful livers from a farm down around the Otways, which is the same region where we get our walnuts.

Duck liver parfait

100 g (3½ oz) butter
275 g (9½ oz) cream
2 shallots, roughly sliced
3 garlic cloves, peeled
5 g (⅛ oz) thyme
smoking wood chips
175 g (6 oz) duck livers
15 g (½ oz) vegetable oil

To finish

125 g (4½ oz) new-season walnuts
60 g (2 oz) Pickled black walnuts
   (page 117)
2 g (¹⁄₁₆ oz) thyme leaves
20 g (¾ oz) walnut oil
20 g (¾ oz) sherry vinegar

Duck liver parfait

Gently heat the butter until melted, then leave to cool at room temperature. Place the cream, shallots, garlic and thyme into a pot and bring to the boil. Remove and leave to cool to room temperature then strain through a fine-mesh sieve. Set up a hot smoker using a similar set up to a steamer: so, a pot, a basket and a lid. Grab some foil and line the bottom of your pot to help with the clean up later. Take your wood chips and lightly wet some of them so that they smoke rather than dry-burn. Put them into the pot on top of the foil. Put the livers into the basket and place the lot over a medium heat. When the chips begin to create enough smoke cover with the lid, knock the heat back a little and smoke for 3 minutes. While this is happening, get a cast-iron pan hot – when the livers have finished smoking transfer them to the pan. Using the vegetable oil, sear on both sides until the livers are medium–rare. Quickly transfer them to an upright blender and blend on high speed. Add the cream and butter mixture. Season to taste, then pass through a fine-mesh sieve into a piping (pastry) bag. Place the bag in an ice bath for at least 4 hours to chill.

To finish

Using a sharp knife finely shave the fresh walnuts then the black walnuts. Put them in a small bowl with the rest of the ingredients and season with salt and black pepper. Give it a gentle mix. Pipe a mound of the parfait into two small serving bowls, grab a spoon and push a divot in the middle of the parfait. Spoon the walnut mix into the hole and serve.

ON SUNDAYS

Condiments and things to eat with cheese

To repeat myself, apart from the crackers, all of this can be done ahead of time. Most of it will even keep in the fridge, meaning you'll get multiple cheese boards out of a little bit of work up front. If you're looking for cheese tips, I'm a white mould guy so I can't go past Brillat-Savarin, a hectically bloomy triple-cream brie. So delicious.

Pickled unripe figs

1 kg (2 lb 3 oz) green unripe figs
600 g (1 lb 5 oz) champagne vinegar
400 g (14 oz) sugar
15 cardamon pods
8 allspice berries
40 g (1½ oz) ginger
½ lemon, zest cut into strips
3 bay leaves
1 rosemary sprig

Pickled unripe figs

Find yourself a cake-testing pin and carefully poke a few holes in each of the green figs. This will help them to pickle evenly. Place all of the other ingredients in a pot with 2 kg (4 lb 6 oz) water and warm over a medium heat until the sugar dissolves. At this point you will need to season the water pretty heavily with salt. Add the figs and place something on top that will keep them submerged, like a lid from a smaller pot. Bring to a gentle simmer and cook until just soft, around 20 minutes. Check the seasoning then carefully spoon the figs into a big, clean glass jar, then pour over the hot pickling liquid. Put the lid on, invert the jar and leave to cool. To serve, slice each fig in half.

Bread and butter pickled cucumbers

6 large cucumbers
2 onions, peeled
175 g (6 oz) table salt
700 g (1 lb 9 oz) white vinegar
300 g (10½ oz) champagne vinegar
150 g (5½ oz) sugar
2 bay leaves
2 tablespoons caraway seeds

Bread and butter pickled cucumbers

Using a sharp knife or a mandolin, cut the cucumbers and onions into 2 mm (1/16 in) thick slices. Grab a container large enough to hold the water and cucumbers. Pour in 1.25 kg (2 lb 12 oz) water and add the salt. Mix until dissolved then add the sliced cucumbers and onion. Make sure everything is submerged and leave to brine for 1 hour. While this is happening get a pot and add the rest of the ingredients. Warm this over a medium heat until you get to around 65°C (149°F), then remove from the heat and leave to cool. Once the pickle brine is cool enough that it won't cook the cucumbers, drain off the salt brine and add into the pickle liquid. Cover and refrigerate.

Oat and rosemary crispbread

100 g (3½ oz) oats
50 g (1¾ oz) sourdough starter
130 g (4½ oz) baker's flour
140 g (5 oz) plain (all-purpose) flour
7 g (¼ oz) salt
5 g (⅛ oz) rosemary leaves

Oat and rosemary crispbread

Preheat both a normal oven to 180°C (350F) and a wood-fired oven to 450°C (842°F). Put the oats on a baking tray and bake in your normal oven until lightly golden brown. Transfer them to a pot and add 250 g (9 oz) water then cook over a low heat until the oats have softened. Leave to cool. To make the dough, add the softened oats, remaining ingredients and 90 g (3 oz) water into the bowl of a stand mixer fitted with a dough hook attachment. Mix on low until the dough comes together then turn it off. Remove the dough from the bowl and wrap in biodegradable plastic wrap. Leave to rest for 1 hour. When the dough is rested, cut off a portion and roll it out as thin as you can using a rolling pin or a pasta machine. Cook the crispbread sheets on the floor of the hot wood oven. This will only take 30 seconds or so.

A Sunday after
a tough week

When I'm feeling cooked, all I want to eat is steak and veggies. I'll cook up a big bit of beef, blanch a heap of broccoli and hit it with some olive oil, salt and pepper. Whether it's the iron or some kind of nostalgic factor, there's something about this combination that picks me up off the mat, and I often find myself craving it before I've properly noticed how exhausted I am.

This lunch is a fair bit fancier than the version Tired Me makes at home, but it's mostly based on the same cravings. And, like all comfort meals should, it ends with a nice helping of ice cream.

Serves 4

(1)   Beef with pepper sauce

(2)   Roast broccoli, lemon, sunflower seed miso

(3)   Heirloom radicchio, sherry vinegar and almond XO

(4)   Bitter orange ice cream, wattleseed and orange blossom

ON SUNDAYS

Beef with pepper sauce

Steak cooked over fire. So simple and yet so, so satisfying. Here we're serving it with a light take on a classic peppercorn sauce – a little brandy, cream, dark vinegar and a mix of different peppercorns. Peppercorn sauce is probably my go-to steak sauce if I'm ordering somewhere, because you rarely go wrong.

Pepper sauce

7 g (¼ oz) black peppercorns

15 g (½ oz) soft green peppercorns

20 g (¾ oz) soft pink peppercorns

100 g (3½ oz) shallot, finely diced

2 garlic cloves, finely diced

25 g (1 oz) vegetable oil

40 g (1½ oz) brandy

3 g (¹⁄₁₀ oz) thyme leaves

30 g (1 oz) Dijon mustard

400 g (14 oz) Beef stock (page 225)

30 g (1 oz) cream

5 g (⅛ oz) stout beer vinegar,
or dark vinegar

To finish

2 × 350 g (12½ oz) scotch fillet steaks

Pepper sauce

Place the black peppercorns and a pinch of salt into a mortar and pestle and crush the peppercorns into a coarse consistency. Put the shallot and garlic in a small pot with the vegetable oil and sweat over a medium–low heat for around 3 minutes, then turn the heat up and add the brandy. Cook until reduced by half then add all the remaining ingredients except the cream and vinegar. Bring to a simmer and cook until everything comes together, around 20 minutes. Finish with the cream and season to taste with salt and a touch of the vinegar.

To finish

Light a fire and let the wood burn down to a good bed of coals. This will take roughly 45 minutes. Pull the steaks out of the fridge and let them come up to an ambient temperature. This is the single best thing you can do when cooking thick steaks like these. Season the steaks liberally with salt then place them, presentation side down, on a rack over the fire. You want to position them in a spot that is hot but not rippingly hot, as it is going to take a little while to get the heat through these guys. Cook for 5–6 minutes then flip them over. Cook the second side for 4–5 minutes, then pull them off the fire and leave to rest, loosely covered with foil, in a warm spot for 5 minutes. Carve with a sharp knife, transfer to a serving dish and cover liberally with the pepper sauce.

Roast broccoli, lemon, sunflower seed miso

This dish may seem modest (and it is), but it's an early Embla example of how direct and simple cooking with fire can be. It's also pretty close to my heart. The magic of a wood-fired oven is that you don't need to do a lot of stuff. Cook the broccoli with care, toss with a little lemon dressing and send it out on a bed of nutty sunflower savouriness.

Sunflower seed miso

80 g (2¾ oz) sunflower seeds
25 g (1 oz) broad bean miso
    or white miso
75 g (2¾ oz) vegetable oil

Lemon dressing

30 g (1 oz) lemon juice
10 g (¼ oz) chardonnay vinegar
2 g (¹⁄₁₆ oz) salt
2 g (¹⁄₁₆ oz) sugar
100 g (3½ oz) olive oil

To finish

1 very large head of broccoli, halved
vegetable oil

Sunflower seed miso

Place the sunflower seeds, miso and 150 g (5½ oz) water in an upright blender. Blend on high speed until the seeds break down, then slowly add the vegetable oil until smooth and emulsified. Season to taste with salt.

Lemon dressing

Blend everything together with 10 g (¼ oz) water using a hand-held blender.

To finish

Preheat a wood-fired oven to 450°C (842°F). Fill a pot with water and bring it to the boil. Season with salt. Set up a bowl of iced water. Cook the broccoli until the stem is tender when poked with a cake-testing pin. Remove straight to the ice bath to stop the cooking process. Once cold, remove and allow the drain thoroughly. When ready to cook, put the halves, cut side up, in a cast-iron pan, lightly oil and season with salt. Put the pan into the wood oven so that the florets are facing the fire. They will have absorbed the most water during blanching so you will need to cook this out to get them crispy. Rotate the pan so that they cook evenly, this will take around 8 minutes. Pull them from the oven and dress with some of the lemon dressing. Spoon some of the sunflower seed cream onto two serving dishes then place the broccoli halves on top.

Heirloom radicchio, sherry vinegar and almond XO

A meaty, winter bitter leaf salad. I love bitter things, especially as a way of balancing out meatiness with freshness. Unlike the majority of salads, which are dressed with a combination of oil and acid, we'll calm down the bitterness and intensity of the radicchio with a strong and savoury sauce that mimics classic Chinese XO.

Almond XO

150 g (5½ oz) almonds, skin on
140 g (5 oz) vegetable oil
30 g (1 oz) shallots, finely sliced
30 g (1 oz) garlic cloves, finely sliced
5 g (⅛ oz) Chinese fermented black beans
10 g (¼ oz) nutritional yeast flakes
1 g (¹⁄₃₂ oz) chilli flakes
1 g (¹⁄₃₂ oz) rosemary leaves
30 g (1 oz) olive oil
40 g (1½ oz) Fermented cabbage juice
　　(see page 225)

To finish

1 head of radicchio
sherry vinegar

Almond XO

Preheat your oven to 180°C (350°F). Put the almonds on a baking tray and cook until only very lightly toasted. Remove them from the oven and let cool. Once cool, give them a good chop through with a knife. Place the vegetable oil in a small pot and warm to around 140°C (285°F). Working in batches, fry off the shallot and then the garlic until lightly golden. Once they're both fried, return to the pot of oil, adding the almonds, black beans, yeast flakes, chilli and rosemary. Give this all a gentle stir while cooking over a low heat. Finally, take off the heat and leave to cool slightly, then add the olive oil and fermented cabbage juice. Season to taste with salt and black pepper.

To finish

Separate the leaves of the radicchio and wash really well under cold water, then spin dry using a salad spinner. Place the leaves into a mixing bowl and spoon over a generous amount of the almond XO. Season with salt and black pepper then add enough sherry vinegar to create a balanced dressing. Mix thoroughly using your hands and transfer to a serving dish.

ON SUNDAYS

Bitter orange ice cream, wattleseed and orange blossom

This bitter orange ice cream is built inside individual cups made from frozen half-orange shells. It's a little bit bougie, but that's OK because we're celebrating a fruit that really doesn't get enough attention. Wormwood, which I use to make vermouth, provides bitterness and tempers the sweetness of the whole dish.

Orange and wormwood ice cream

500 g (1 lb 2 oz) orange juice
(from around 4 oranges)
zest of 2 oranges
300 g (10½ oz) cream
80 g (2¾ oz) sugar
1 g (⅟₃₂ oz) wormwood
(available from health food stores)
6 egg yolks

Brown butter salted caramel

60 g (2 oz) unsalted butter
70 g (2½ oz) cream
120 g (4½ oz) sugar
40 g (1½ oz) water

Orange and wormwood ice cream

Using the oranges allocated for the juice, take two and cut in half horizontally. Using a spoon, scoop out the flesh and keep this for squeezing your juice. Take the from four half-orange shells and place them in the freezer for later on. Take a small pot and add half the orange zest, the cream, half the sugar and the wormwood. Fit a stand mixer with a whisk attachment and prepare a bowl of iced water. Put the egg yolks in the bowl along with the remaining sugar and zest. Whisk this mix on high speed until light and creamy. Put the pot over a low heat and warm until the sugar dissolves, then turn it up to high. When it reaches a heavy boil, quickly turn the mixer down a little and pour in the cream so that the heat cooks the yolks through. Continue to mix for 5 minutes, then slowly pour in the orange juice. Cool the mixture over the ice bath, then pass through a fine-mesh sieve. Freeze in an ice-cream machine according to the manufacturer's instructions.

Brown butter salted caramel

Place the butter in a small pot and warm over a low heat until it melts. Turn the heat up and cook the butter through to a dark golden brown. When it is smelling delicious and is about to go too far, pour in the cream to stop the cooking process, then remove from the heat. In another small pot combine the sugar and 40 g (1½ oz) water and warm this over a low heat so that the sugar dissolves evenly. Increase the heat and cook the sugar until it begins to turn a light golden brown. At this point, slow the heat down a little. The sugar will still keep cooking rapidly, but it will be easier to stop it at the right point if it is moving a little slower. Cook until it reaches a deep dark-brown caramel. You want it to be on the very edge of bitterness here. When you're happy with the colour, very carefully pour in the cream mix and emulsify together. Leave to cool slightly and season to taste with salt. Chill to set.

Continued next page →

Wattleseed chocolate

125 g (4½ oz) white chocolate callets

12 g (½ oz) ground toasted wattleseed

Milk streusel pastry

60 g (2 oz) butter

50 g (1¾ oz) sugar

1 g (1/32 oz) salt

40 g (1½ oz) cornflour (cornstarch)

60 g (2 oz) skim-milk powder

35 g (1¼ oz) plain (all-purpose) flour

Orange-blossom ganache

2 g (1/16 oz) gelatine sheets

75 g (2¾ oz) white chocolate callets

50 g (1¾ oz) milk

70 g (2½ oz) cream

3 g (1/10 oz) orange-blossom water

To finish

10 g (¼ oz) thyme leaves

Wattleseed chocolate	Preheat the oven to 160°C (320°F). Place the white chocolate and wattleseed into a metal mixing bowl and place in the oven. After 5 minutes the chocolate will melt, so give it a quick stir to incorporate the wattleseed. Cook until the chocolate caramelises and turns a deep brown colour, around 30 minutes. You will need to stir it a few times during this process. Once it's nice and dark, remove it from the oven and transfer to a container and chill. It will set pretty hard, so take a knife and finely chop it through.
Milk streusel pastry	Fit a stand mixer with a paddle attachment. Place the butter, sugar and salt in the bowl and beat on high speed until the butter creams nicely. Sift the dry ingredients through a fine-mesh sieve then add to the bowl with the butter mix. Mix on low speed until it forms a loose-flowing powdery consistency. Chill. Yes, this pastry is uncooked – it's way better this way!
Orange-blossom ganache	Place the gelatine sheets in a small bowl and cover with cold water. Leave for 5 minutes then, once softened, drain and squeeze out any excess water. Place the white chocolate in a small bowl. Heat the milk in a small pot to just under a boil, add the softened gelatine and swirl until it melts through. Pour this hot mixture onto the white chocolate callets and let the heat melt them through. When melted, use a hand-held blender to blend it until smooth, then pour in the cold cream and orange-blossom water and blend until incorporated. Transfer the ganache to a piping (pastry) bag and chill to set, preferably overnight if you can.
To finish	Take the four frozen orange shells and spoon a couple of lumps of the brown butter salted caramel into the bottom of each. Next, pipe in a little of the orange-blossom ganache, then sprinkle in a spoon of the milk pastry, the wattleseed chocolate and a little thyme. Finally, scoop two spoons of ice cream on top and smooth flat with a palette knife. These will hold for a while in the freezer so you can make them one by one, if that's less stressful?!

A citrus season Sunday

One of the silver linings of winter setting in is citrus coming into season. These days, we expect to get citrus fruits all throughout the year (and we get annoyed when lemons hit $2 a pop at the height of summer), but winter is when citrus is at its freshest and, as always, fresh is best. When you think about the array of sweet, high, refreshing and bright notes citrus contributes to our experience of food, you start to understand why it's not weird that I have a folder of Google Maps screenshots on my phone showing the locations of different citrus trees around town. Citrus is life.

At Embla, we use the winter months to put down as many preserves of yuzu, bergamot, blood orange, lemon, tangelo and cumquat that we can to use throughout the year. This menu leans into these preserves, as well as the gorgeous fresh stuff.

Serves 4

(1)   Mussels, hispi cabbage, hazelnut and yuzu

(2)   Gurnard, orange and coriander seed

(3)   Creamed corn, dried citrus, marjoram and crème fraîche

(4)   Bergamot sherbet, lemonade fruit, white chocolate and peanut

Mussels, hispi cabbage, hazelnut and yuzu

Mussels pair well with wintery savoury things like hazelnuts and charred cabbage. That may seem counterintuitive but the sum of the parts is much better than you'd expect. The light pickle on the mussels makes them deliciously tender, which combined with the soft-yet-cold cooked cabbage, crunchy hazelnuts and brightness from the yuzu, you get a super tasty and textural dish.

Mussels

500 g (1 lb 2 oz) small mussels
¼ fennel bulb, finely diced
2 garlic cloves, finely diced
20 g (¾ oz) vegetable oil
sherry vinegar

Hazelnut pesto

100 g (3½ oz) hazelnuts, skin on
½ shallot, finely diced
2 g (¹⁄₁₆ oz) nutritional yeast flakes
zest of ¼ orange
2 g (¹⁄₁₆ oz) thyme leaves
50 g (1¾ oz) hazelnut oil
50 g (1¾ oz) vegetable oil
20 g (¾ oz) Fermented cabbage juice
     (see page 225)
1 garlic clove, peeled

Hispi cabbage

1 medium-sized hispi cabbage,
     or sugarloaf cabbage
20 g (¾ oz) vegetable oil

To finish

10 g (¼ oz) olive oil
15 g (½ oz) preserved yuzu skins, sliced

Mussels

Bring a pot of water up to a simmer and place a colander inside a bowl for the cooked mussels. Working in three or four batches, quickly blanch the mussels in the simmering water just until the shells crack open, remove and place in the colander to drain. Discard any that don't open. Once you have blanched all the mussels place them in the fridge to chill. Reserve the liquid that collects at the bottom of the bowl and a little of the blanching water. Place the fennel and garlic in a clean pot with the vegetable oil and sweat gently over a low heat until softened. Strain the mussel liquor through a fine-mesh sieve and add to the fennel pot. Bring this to the boil, skim well and simmer until you are happy with the flavour intensity. Pass the liquid through a fine-mesh sieve again and chill. Remove the mussels from their shells and pull away the beard. Once the liquid is cold add the mussels and season to taste with sherry vinegar.

Hazelnut pesto

Preheat the oven to 180°C (350°F). Place the hazelnuts on a baking tray and toast until only lightly golden, then remove and let cool slightly. Roughly chop through the hazelnuts, making sure to keep the skins, and transfer to a mixing bowl with the shallot. Add all the other ingredients except the garlic. Give it all a solid mix, then grate in the garlic using a microplane, to taste. Season with salt and black pepper.

Hispi cabbage

Preheat a wood-fired oven to 450°C (842°F). Peel off any unwanted outer cabbage leaves and keep them to make fermented cabbage juice (see page 225). Using a knife cut the cabbage in half lengthways and check that it is clean inside. Place both halves in a cast-iron pan, add the oil and season with salt. Roast the cabbage on all sides until it begins to soften. This will take around 8–10 minutes – you may need to add a touch of water to the pan during the cook to create some steam, which will aid the cooking process. When they're cooked, remove from the oven and place on a tray, cut side down, to cool. When cool, peel off the top three or four layers and lay flat on a cutting board. Use a knife to cut 5 mm (¼ in) wide slices. Take the inner core and cut it into bite-sized pieces.

To finish

Take the mussels and, using a sharp knife, cut them in half then place them into a small mixing bowl. Add the cooked cabbage insides, olive oil and the preserved yuzu. Season with salt and black pepper and give it a gentle mix. Divide between two serving bowls, then spoon some of the hazelnut pesto over both. Finally, lay over the slices of cabbage to cover.

Gurnard, orange and coriander seed

Whole fish over the fire – chef's kiss. And what a beautiful fish gurnard is – both in looks and the way it eats. You've got that handsome orange and white body with the incredible blue, butterfly-esque fins. And then when you cook it, it stays firm without being tough, and it flakes perfectly. Here we pair it with a coriander seed butter – there's so much flavour in the seeds – and finish with a little orange zest and juice.

Coriander seed butter

10 g (¼ oz) coriander seeds
1 garlic clove, peeled
125 g (4½ oz) unsalted butter

To finish

2 × 1 kg (2 lb 3 oz) whole gurnards
150 g (5½ oz) Fish skin stock (page 225)
1 orange

Coriander seed butter

Put the coriander seeds in a small pan and toast over a medium heat until fragrant, then remove and let cool slightly. Grind to a fine powder using a mortar and pestle. Add the garlic and a healthy pinch of salt, then grind to a smooth paste. Lastly, add the butter and work it through.

To finish

This is another recipe where knowing how to butterfly a whole fish comes in handy. Alternatively, you could ask your fishmonger nicely to do this for you. Lay the gurnard on a cutting board with the belly side facing you. Using a sharp knife cut horizontally along the spine from the end of the belly opening to the tail. Carefully work your knife up to the top of the spine bones making sure to cut through near the top of the back. Repeat this on the other side. Remove the head and lay the fish resting on its back so that the fillets splay open. Using a pair of kitchen scissors, cut along the spine bones as close to the skin as you can. Again, using the scissors, trim the dorsal and pectoral fins as they will burn while getting grilled. Using your knife again, cut away the ribcage bones and then remove any pin bones with a pair of fish tweezers.

Light a good fire and let it burn down to a solid bed of coals. When ready to cook, lightly oil and season both sides of the fish and lay flat in a fish grilling cage. Place the fish over the coals, skin side down, and grill until evenly golden. You may need to move the fish into a higher position over the fire to finish cooking it through without overly charring. When just done, remove from the cage and transfer to a serving plate. For the sauce, put the fish stock and two good spoonfuls of the coriander seed butter into a small pot to warm through. When warmed enough, season the sauce with salt, microplaned orange zest and a touch of orange juice. Spoon the sauce over the fish and serve.

ON SUNDAYS

ON SUNDAYS

Creamed corn, dried citrus, marjoram and crème fraîche

This is an OG Embla dish which you could also make in summer, but it's so smooth and comforting that it also makes perfect sense in winter. Corn, onion, a little cream (not much at all) blitzed and cooked out until soft, then finished with a little butter. Simple, right? But there's something about how sweet and rich it becomes that I still don't really understand. Calm it all down with the toppings: sour crème fraîche, a dried citrus crumb, bitter onion ash and fragrant marjoram.

Creamed corn base
10 corn cobs or 1 kg (2 lb 3 oz) frozen corn
1 onion, peeled
100 g (3½ oz) cream

Dried citrus
½ orange
1 lemon
1 lime

Burnt onion
1 onion
20 g (¾ oz) vegetable oil

To finish
30 g (1 oz) unsalted butter
50 g (1¾ oz) crème fraîche
15 g (½ oz) marjoram leaves

Creamed corn base

You will need a steam oven to cook the corn base or, failing that, a sous-vide bath. Preheat the oven to 100 per cent steam and 90°C (194°F). Using a knife, cut the kernels away from each corn cob and transfer to a large bowl blender. Give the kernels a quick pulse to break them down a little. Tip this into a bowl and add the cream. Use a sharp knife to finely dice the onion as small as you can, then add to the bowl with the corn. Season well with salt, then seal inside a vacuum-pack bag on high pressure. Smooth the bag flat to help the base cook evenly and place in the oven to cook for 1½ hours. When finished, cool in an ice bath.

Dried citrus

This is a great way to use the parts of your citrus left over from the zesting jobs. Using a sharp knife cut away all of the skin and pith, leaving a clean inner core. Cut the core into thin slices and lay them out on a dehydrator tray or, failing that, a baking paper-lined oven tray. Dry on as low a temperature as you can overnight; they will take a lot to dry right out and you may need to flip them over to give them a helping hand. When they're crisp, chop them as finely as you can and combine. Store in an airtight container until ready to use.

Burnt onion

Preheat your wood-fired oven to 450°C (842°F). Peel the onion and cut into fine rings. Place them into a bowl, add the oil and season with salt. Lay the onions on a baking tray and cook in the wood oven until burnt and black all of the way through then remove to cool. Finally, chop them into a powder using a knife.

To finish

Place the creamed corn base into a cast-iron pot and warm in the wood-fired oven, add the butter towards the end and season with salt to taste. Divide the corn into two serving bowls and scoop a spoon of the crème fraîche into the middle of each. Next, scatter the marjoram leaves around and then sprinkle the dried citrus over that. Finally, top with a scattering of the burnt onion powder.

ON SUNDAYS

Bergamot sherbet, lemonade fruit, white chocolate and peanut

The oil extracted from bergamot skins is what's used to flavour Earl Grey tea, and the fruit itself is unlike any other citrus you've eaten. Somewhere between a Meyer lemon and a grapefruit or bitter orange, it's incredibly aromatic and strong, and robust enough to stand up to a lot of different flavour combinations. We use the fruit to make gallons of ice cream and dry the skins and cores to use whenever an otherworldly fragrant hit is needed. You will need to begin this recipe a day ahead.

Bergamot sherbet

500 g (1 lb 2 oz) milk
zest of ¼ bergamot
100 g (3½ oz) sugar
100 g (3½ oz) bergamot juice

Peanut ganache

50 g (1¾ oz) peanuts, skin off
100 g (3½ oz) milk
300 g (10½ oz) cream
2 g (¹⁄₁₆ oz) gelatine sheet
150 g (5½ oz) white chocolate callets

Soft peanuts

100 g (3½ oz) peanuts, skin off
50 g (1¾ oz) sugar

To finish

2 lemonade fruit
10 g (¼ oz) virgin peanut oil

Bergamot sherbet

Place the milk, bergamot zest and sugar in a small pot and warm up to around 60°C (140°F) to dissolve the sugar. Pour this into a container and chill overnight to infuse. The following day, strain the zest out with a fine-mesh sieve and mix in the fresh bergamot juice. Freeze in an ice-cream machine according to the manufacturer's instructions.

Peanut ganache

Preheat the oven to 180°C (350°F). Place the peanuts on a baking tray and bake until very lightly golden brown. Place the milk and half the peanuts in a small pot and bring to the boil, then leave to cool at room temperature before straining through a fine-mesh sieve. Put the cream and the other half of the peanuts into a small pot and warm to 65°C (149°F). Pour into a container and chill overnight. Strain through a fine-mesh sieve and keep cold. Place the gelatine sheet in a small bowl and cover with cold water. Leave for 5 minutes, or until softened, then drain and squeeze off any excess water. Put the white chocolate in a small bowl then put the milk into a small pot and bring up to the boil. Add in the softened gelatine and swirl to melt through. Pour the milk mix onto the chocolate and let it melt for a few minutes. Using a hand-held blender, blend the chocolate mix until smooth then pour in the infused cream and blend until incorporated. Transfer into a piping (pastry) bag and chill overnight.

Soft peanuts

Place the peanuts and sugar into the bowl of a pressure cooker with 200 g (7 oz) water and stir until the sugar dissolves. Put the lid on and cook under pressure for 30 minutes. Let the pressure off and transfer the softened peanuts and syrup to a container and chill.

To finish

Take the lemonade fruit and cut two cheeks off either side of each fruit. Lay the cheeks down and cut them into as fine slices as you can. Grab two serving bowls and spoon some of the soft peanuts into the bottom of each. Next, scoop in a big wedge of the bergamot sherbet and sit it on top of the peanuts. Pipe some of the peanut ganache over the top of the sherbet and then, working one by one, cover this with the slices of lemonade fruit. Spoon a little of the peanut oil over the top.

A spice odyssey Sunday

Just as in summer we seek lightness and freshness, in winter we crave bigness. Bigness, though, can be confused with heaviness – cream, starch, syrup – which is kind of a poor-man's interesting. The 'big' you want should come from flavour, and the quickest route to that is through spice. There's something about spice that we interpret as dark and mysterious, so it really is a winter idea.

An important disclaimer is that at Embla we don't use a lot of hot spices. Heat is just one facet of spice and, given a lot of what we serve is inadvertently Mediterranean, we rarely trouble the Scoville scale. Instead, we focus on singular spice profiles, avoiding muddy melanges in favour of clarity. If we serve a peach, it should taste like a peach. The same goes for spices. The recipes below each approach the idea of spice with this clarity in mind.

Serves 4

(1)   Preserved chicken, yuzu, kale and pine nut

(2)   Skate, macadamia cream, shiitake and wattleseed

(3)   Potato cous cous, lemon, vadouvan and summer savoury

(4)   Dried fig tart, quince, chocolate and coriander
        seed ice cream

Preserved chicken, yuzu, kale and pine nut

This might sound a little odd, but it's a riff on an Italian method for preserving rabbit called tonno di coniglio, which translates as rabbit tuna. Basically you boil the meat and submerge it in oil, which keeps everything sterile and also permeates the flesh, giving it a luxurious tinned tuna texture, hence the name. The garlic here provides the spice component. Blanched, dried over fire, and grated over the dish – it's almost a garlic version of smoked paprika. You will need to begin parts of this recipe around a week ahead.

Preserved chicken
2 chicken breasts
2 garlic cloves, peeled
1 rosemary sprig
40 g (1½ oz) oregano leaves
400 g (14 oz) olive oil

Pine nut milk
50 g (1¾ oz) pine nuts
xanthan gum

Dried garlic
10 garlic cloves, peeled

To finish
20 g (¾ oz) pine nuts
½ teaspoon diced shallot
100 g (3½ oz) baby purple kale leaves
10 g (¼ oz) preserved yuzu oil
5 g (⅛ oz) lemon juice
2 g (1/16 oz) dried yuzu core, chopped (you can find dried yuzu at gourmet food stores)

Preserved chicken

Using a sharp knife, trim each chicken breast of any sinew and then place in a small pot with all of the other ingredients. Season liberally with salt and warm over a low heat until the temperature comes up to 60°C (140°F). You will need to maintain this temperature for 1 hour and 10 minutes. This will ensure the chicken is cooked through but in a very gentle way. Once the time is up, remove the pan from the heat and leave to cool to room temperature. When it has cooled, remove the chicken and, using your hands, shred it down into bite-sized chunks. Place these into a clean container. Take the olive oil and strain it through a fine-mesh sieve into the container with the shredded chicken. Refrigerate this for a minimum of 5 days or upwards of 2 weeks. Be very careful of hygiene through this process to ensure nothing goes awry. The prolonged aging produces an incredibly tender protein that will resemble good-quality tinned tuna.

Pine nut milk

Preheat the oven to 180°C (350°F). Place the pine nuts on a baking tray and bake for 4 minutes, or until only just beginning to take on some colour. Transfer them to an upright blender with 250 g (9 oz) water and blend on high speed until the water warms up to around 50°C (122°F). You will be able to feel the temperature change with your hand on the side of the blender bowl. Pour the nut milk into a container and chill overnight. The following day, pass the liquid through a fine-mesh sieve, season with salt and thicken slightly using a hand-held blender and a very small amount of xanthan gum (around 0.001 g).

Dried garlic

Place the garlic cloves in a small pot and cover with cold water. Bring this up to a boil then drain off the hot water. Repeat this cycle five times. After the final blanch, take the cloves and place them on a small rack and dry them over a wood fire for 2–3 days.

To finish

Drain off the preserved shredded chicken and place into a small mixing bowl. Season with salt and black pepper. Divide the chicken between two serving bowls then scatter the fresh pine nuts and diced shallot over the top. Spoon in some of the pine nut milk then a little of the yuzu oil. Put the baby kale leaves into a small bowl and dress with some yuzu oil and lemon juice. Season, then arrange them on top of the chicken mix. Finally, sprinkle some of the dried yuzu powder over then use a microplane to finely grate the dried garlic over everything.

ON SUNDAYS

Skate, macadamia cream, shiitake and wattleseed

This is a cool bit of technique, steaming fish in a wood-fired oven to keep it delicate. Skate can be tricky to cook – its lack of intramuscular fat makes it particularly unforgiving, which is why you don't see it on many menus. But done right (you've got this), the flesh has a meaty denseness that's absolutely unreal. Wattleseed adds a roasty, nutty spiciness.

Skate

1 small skate wing

Macadamia cream

100 g (3½ oz) macadamia nuts
20 g (¾ oz) broad bean miso,
    or white miso
¼ garlic clove, peeled
50 g (1¾ oz) vegetable oil
100 g (3½ oz) Fish skin stock (page 225)

Wattleseed powder

50 g (1¾ oz) toasted wattle seeds
1 g (1/32 oz) salt

To finish

vegetable oil
10 shiitake mushrooms, diced
20 g (¾ oz) Cherry blossom vinegar
    (see page 225)
50 g (1¾ oz) Fish skin stock (page 225)
1 garlic clove, peeled
5 g (⅛ oz) basil leaves

Skate

I really enjoy prepping skate wings; they have a piece of cartilage that divides the flesh into top and bottom, so it already has a natural guide to how you need to cut it. Lay the skate wing flat on a cutting board and, using a sharp knife, start at the thick square end. Run your knife flat along the cartilage in long even cuts all the way to the wing tip. Repeat on the other side. Trim away any flesh that is too thin. We will cook each half as they are, so you need to think about how the thinnest end will cook in regard to the thickest.

Macadamia cream

Place everything except the fish stock in an upright blender. Starting on a slow speed, blend until smooth then turn the speed up and slowly add 100 g (3½ oz) water and the stock until you reach a smooth, thin-ish puree consistency.

Wattleseed powder

Blend wattle seeds and salt together in a spice grinder until you have a fine powder.

To finish

Preheat a wood-fired oven to 450°C (842°F). Heat a cast-iron skillet in the wood oven then add a little vegetable oil and the diced mushrooms and season with salt. Roast them in the oven for 4 minutes or so. Once they're nicely caramelised and cooked through, pull the pan from the oven and season them with the cherry blossom vinegar.

To cook the skate, slightly oil and season both sides of the fillet then place into a soaked terracotta dish. Add the stock, garlic and basil leaves. Cover with a lid and cook in the wood oven for around 5–6 minutes, depending on the thickness of your fillet. The key word here is gentle: gentle heat and a gentle cook. Skate isn't a friendly piece of fish to cook, so go lightly with the heat. Grab two serving plates and scoop two spoons of the macadamia cream into the middle of them. Cover the cream with the roasted shiitakes then dust with some of the wattleseed powder. Lastly, place the skate on top.

Potato cous cous, lemon, vadouvan and summer savoury

I had this on the menu at my old restaurant and the chefs there hated me for it. Fortunately, making it at home is much more manageable than cranking out a tonne of it in a commercial context. The result is undeniably tasty – tiny beads of tender potato dressed in a vadouvan butter. Vadouvan is a lovely spice blend that's so warm and friendly. It freezes really well so make a big batch. You may want to start this recipe a day ahead to hang the yoghurt.

Lemon yoghurt

150 g (5½ oz) unsweetened yoghurt

1 lemon

Vadouvan spice

80 g (2¾ oz) vegetable oil

400 g (14 oz) shallots, finely minced

70 g (2½ oz) garlic, finely minced

30 g (1 oz) onion, finely minced

50 g (1¾ oz) ginger, finely minced

7 g (¼ oz) curry leaves, finely sliced

7 g (¼ oz) yellow mustard seeds

2 g (¹⁄₁₆ oz) ground turmeric

5 g (⅛ oz) Madras curry powder

4 g (⅛ oz) salt

3 g (¹⁄₁₀ oz) ground cumin

4 g (⅛ oz) ground coriander seeds

4 g (⅛ oz) fenugreek seeds

2 g (¹⁄₁₆ oz) black pepper

1 g (¹⁄₃₂ oz) ground cardamom

1 g (¹⁄₃₂ oz) ground nutmeg

2 cloves, ground

Vadouvan brown butter

200 g (7 oz) unsalted butter

35 g (1¼ oz) vadouvan spice (see above)

Potato couscous

1 kg (2 lb 3 oz) Dutch cream potatoes

To finish

25 g (1 oz) sunflower seeds, toasted

25 g (1 oz) pumpkin seeds (pepitas), toasted

10 g (¼ oz) dried summer savoury

Lemon yoghurt

Very gently pour the yoghurt into a fine-mesh sieve and hang above a container overnight in your fridge. The following day take the thickened yoghurt and put it in a small bowl. Use a microplane to grate in a little lemon zest and squeeze in some juice. Season with salt and adjust accordingly; you want it to be sour, bright and salty.

Vadouvan spice

Preheat the oven to 70°C (158°F). Heat the oil in a cast-iron pan and add the shallot, garlic and onion. Cook this over a medium heat for around 20 minutes, making sure to stir the whole way through so it doesn't catch too badly. Add the ginger, curry leaves and mustard seeds and cook for another 5 minutes. You want this mix to caramelise slightly, so don't be afraid to turn the heat up a little if needs be. Add in the rest of the spices, give it a good stir, and cook for another 5–8 minutes. Transfer the mix over to a baking paper-lined baking tray and place into the low oven for 3–4 hours, or until dried out a little. Any excess is best kept in the freezer or an airtight bag.

Vadouvan brown butter

Grab a small pot, put the butter into it and place it over a low heat until the butter melts. When it has, turn the heat up and cook it until the butter turns a nutty brown and smells delicious. Add the vadouvan and give it a good blend using a hand-held blender, then season to taste with salt.

Potato couscous

Peel the potatoes so that there are no blemishes left, then cut into rough dice. Put the potato into a bowl blender and add a splash or water. Blend the potato on high until the texture breaks down to a fine, cous cous-sized crumb. Set a fine-mesh sieve over a small bucket and place the whole set up into your sink. Tip the potato crumb into the sieve and proceed to wash it under cold running water. What this is doing is rinsing the starch from the potato, which will give it a better texture later in the game. When the water is running clear, let the potato drain and then press off as much moisture as you can. When you are ready to cook, set up a steaming scenario. So, a pot of boiling water and a lid. Give the potato a fluff so that it will cook evenly then put the sieve into the steamer pot and cover. Steam for about 8 minutes, or until the potato has just cooked through.

To finish

Scoop some of the lemon yoghurt onto a serving dish. Put the hot potato cous cous into a small bowl, season with salt and add the seeds and savoury. Give it a gentle mix then scoop it on top of the yoghurt. Lastly, dress this with the vadouvan butter.

Dried fig tart, quince, chocolate and coriander seed ice cream

The roasted coriander seed ice cream is the eye opener here, with so much complexity from only one spice. For me, chocolate desserts are normally so strong and rich and boring. This is so textural and the flavour combo is varied and interesting. From the tart shell – built from dried figs, macadamia nuts and chocolate biscuits – to the chocolate ganache, poached quince and super-flavourful ice cream. It's another dish that I absolutely love.

Tart shell

50 g (1¾ oz) dried figs, finely diced

50 g (1¾ oz) macadamia nuts, finely diced

100 g (3½ oz) Chocolate biscuit
(see page 139), roughly chopped

40 g (1½ oz) brown butter, melted

Coriander seed ice cream

500 g (1 lb 2 oz) milk

350 g (12½ oz) sugar

90 g (3 oz) glucose

400 g (14 oz) cream

35 g (1¼ oz) milk powder

25 g (1 oz) coriander seeds

10 g (¼ oz) locust bean gum

Poached quince

500 g (1 lb 2 oz) water

125 g (4½ oz) sugar

100 g (3½ oz) sherry vinegar

1 vanilla pod

3 bay leaves

1 rosemary sprig

1 quince

Chocolate ganache

2 egg yolks

60 g (2 oz) milk

60 g (2 oz) cream

70 g (2½ oz) dark chocolate callets

Fig leaf vinegar meringue

60 g (2 oz) egg whites

140 g (5 oz) sugar

50 g (1¾ oz) Fig-leaf vinegar
(see page 225)

Tart shell

Put the fig, nut and biscuit into a small bowl and add the melted brown butter, mix to combine. Grab two fluted 8–9 cm (3¼–3½ in) metal tart shells and split the mix between them. Use your hands to press the dough into the tart shell so that it is evenly dispersed and has a hollow centre. Place into a freezer for 20 minutes and then pop them out of the mould. Refrigerate.

Coriander seed ice cream

Place the milk, sugar, glucose, cream and milk powder in a pot and warm over a low heat. Put the coriander seeds into a small pan and toast over a high heat until reasonably dark and fragrant. Leave them to cool slightly then grind into a fine powder using a spice grinder. When the milk mix is warm, add the ground coriander, remove from the heat and leave to infuse for 1 hour. Using a hand-held blender, shear in the locust bean gum until the milk mix thickens and then pass the lot through a fine-mesh sieve. Freeze in an ice-cream machine according to the manufacturer's instructions.

Poached quince

Put everything except the quince into a small pot with 500 g (1 lb 2 oz) and warm to dissolve the sugar. Peel the quince, cut into quarters lengthways then cut away the core. Place the quince in the poaching liquid and cook just under a simmer until soft and rosy pink, around 1 hour. Remove from the heat and chill. Once cold, cut each cheek into 3 mm (⅛ in) slices.

Chocolate ganache

Put the yolks into a small bowl and lightly beat until smooth, then transfer to a small pot with the milk and cream. Cook gently over a low heat until the mix gets to 80°C (176°F), then pour over the dark chocolate callets. Leave to melt for a minute or two, then stir to combine. Transfer into a piping (pastry) bag and chill overnight.

Fig leaf vinegar meringue

Put the egg whites in the bowl of a stand mixer fitted with a whisk attachment. Combine the sugar and 50 g (1¾ oz) water in a small pot and warm over a low heat until the sugar dissolves, then turn the heat up and cook it until it reaches 117°C (243°F). When the sugar is close to temperature, turn the mixer on high then slowly pour the hot sugar down the sides to cook the meringue. Continue to whisk until the meringue cools then add the vinegar. Transfer to a piping (pastry) bag and chill.

To finish

Take a tart shell and pipe a layer of chocolate ganache into the bottom. Cover this with a few slices of the poached quince. Working from the outside in, pipe the vinegar meringue, covering everything. Use a blow torch to thoroughly burn the meringue then scoop a quenelle of the ice cream on top.

Making bread

You could say bread is a big deal at Embla. Every day our wood oven produces twelve loaves of sourdough, each weighing about 1.25 kg (2 lb 12 oz). We use it in a variety of ways, incorporated into a range of dishes or served warm with butter. It's made with a starter that came to Australia in my suitcase when I first moved here 10 or so years ago and prepared using a method very similar to the one you're about to read. I've taught this way of breadmaking to a number of people over the years and all of them have been able to make excellent bread on the second or third bake.

It's a simple thing that's easy to take for granted, but a huge amount of time and focus is put into making our bread. For us and the way we want to do things, it sends a clear message about the care and time we aim to put into all our food. The act of making good bread is so elemental. You're taking flour, water and salt, and transforming it into something so nourishing and profound. It's for these reasons that the task of making those twelve daily loaves is given to the chef running the pass that shift (in other words, the most senior chef in the kitchen).

Like I said, this recipe has been tried and tested. It mitigates the most common downfall for aspiring bread makers, which is overworking the dough. You really don't need to knead your dough to death. It also lets the bread develop a beautiful sourness, which, contrary to popular belief, comes not from the amount of starter you use, but the time you give your starter to do its thing during resting. The process takes some patience and also a bit of restraint, but trust me, the results are pretty damn satisfying.

This recipe assumes you have a sourdough starter ready to go. You can either make your own or buy some from your friendly local baker.

Sourdough

745 g (1 lb 10 oz) lukewarm water

200 g (7 oz) sourdough starter

600 g (1 lb 5 oz) plain (all-purpose) flour, plus
    extra for dusting

415 g (14½ oz) strong baker's flour

25 g (1 oz) salt

(1) OK, so this process is going to take the better part of a day, but only in small time increments, and you can easily work it into an afternoon. Take a wide, medium-to-large bowl and add the lukewarm water. You add the water first for two reasons: firstly, so that the flour doesn't glue itself to the bowl, and secondly, to test that the sourdough starter is alive and active. Add the sourdough starter and it should float in the water. This is because if it is alive it will be producing gas, etc. Lastly,

(2) add your flours. Now rinse your hands to make them

(3,4) damp and, using one hand, give the ingredients a rough mix through. This should only take a minute or so. What you are trying to do here is just roughly disperse the

(5) flour and water so that the flour can hydrate evenly. The temptation is to mix and mix, but this will just toughen

(6) the end texture. Cover with a tea towel (dish towel) and leave to rest for 45 minutes. At this point you've probably realised how annoying it is to get the flour off your hands: pro tip is to leave your hands wet and the dough won't stick as badly.

(7) Mix the salt with 35 g (1¼ oz) water, then pour

(8) this on top of the dough. Use your wet hand to mix again until the dough begins to come together, around 2 minutes. It's a good idea during this mix to feel for any flour clumps and try to crush them. Do not worry about how loose the dough feels at this point – this is what you want. Cover with the towel again and rest for another 45 minutes.

(9-18) The next four steps are essentially the same action, and you will see how the bread develops its structure as you go along. Working with both hands wet, carefully release the dough from the outer edge of

(9) the bowl. With your hands at 9 and 3 on a clock, pick the dough up through the middle. The front and back edges will hang down and you want to encourage this stretching by gently waggling the dough back and forth.

(10) Lower the dough back into the bowl and fold it in half on

(11,12) itself. Turn the bowl 90 degrees and repeat this picking up/stretching/folding process. Cover with the towel and

(13,14) rest for 30 minutes. Repeat this folding process another three times. You will see the dough change from a loose

(15,16) wet mass to something that is smooth and soft but
(17,18) bound together by its own tension. After the final rest
(19) transfer the dough onto a lightly floured benchtop and
(20) cut roughly in half using a dough scraper. Gently shape
(21) into round balls using the dough scraper, lightly dust with flour, cover and rest for 30 minutes.

After this rest, take your two bannetons and lightly dust with flour. Flip the rested dough upside down and

(22) gently stretch it out to a rough triangle shape. Working

(23,24) from the top of the triangle fold it on itself by one-third.

(25) Tuck the left and right sides in again, fold over the final third and pinch the seam together. Pick the dough up

(26) and fold the two ends together into the middle and

(27) pinch again. Place the dough into the banneton seam side up, cover and leave to rest for 15 minutes. Place both bannetons into the fridge overnight.

The following day, turn your oven to 230°C (446°F) fan forced, and place a deep cast-iron pan inside with the lid on. Once the oven and pan are both very, very hot, take one bread out of the fridge and upend onto a

(28,29) square of baking paper. Score the top of the bread in however artistically inspired way you want and then

(30) lower the bread on the paper into the pan. Cover with the lid and bake for 25 minutes. After this, remove the

(31) lid and bake for another 25 minutes. Remove the loaf

(32) and cool on a rack. Put the pot back in to heat again and repeat the cooking process. Here comes the test of will power – you ideally need to let the bread cool slightly so that the structure sets and to help any moisture steam off the fresh loaf.

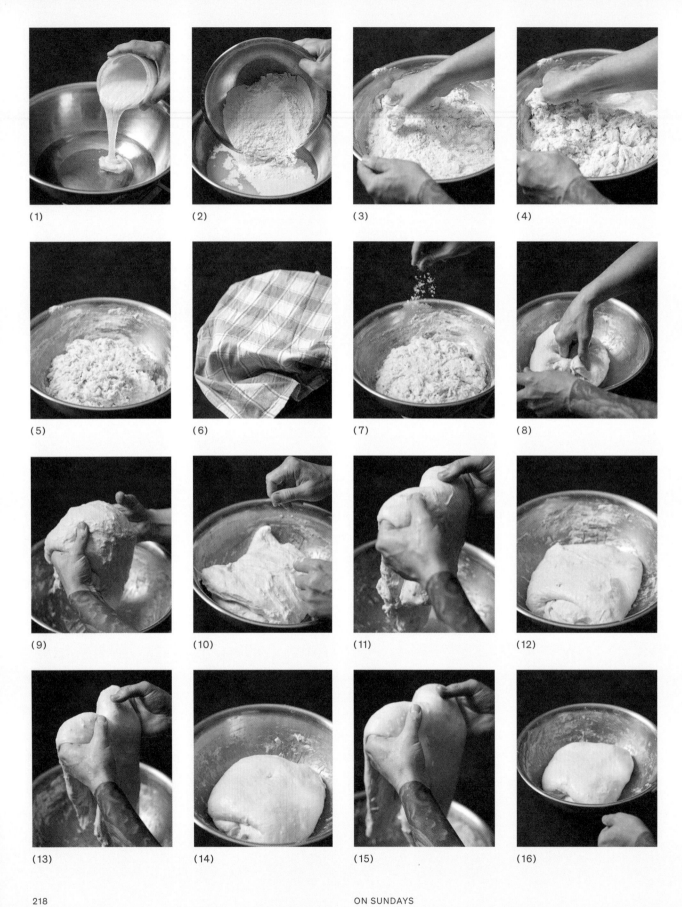

(1)　(2)　(3)　(4)

(5)　(6)　(7)　(8)

(9)　(10)　(11)　(12)

(13)　(14)　(15)　(16)

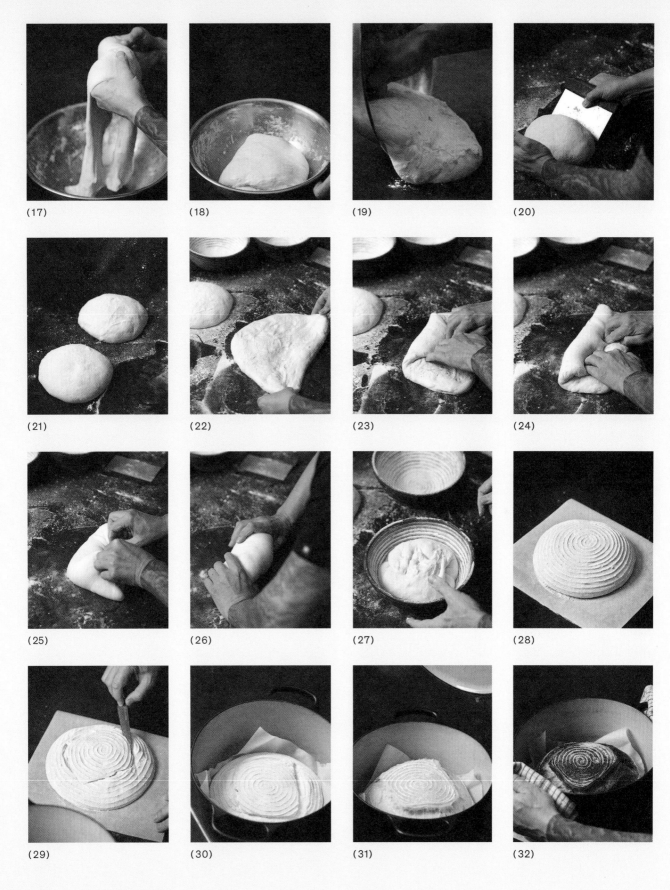

(17)　　　　(18)　　　　(19)　　　　(20)

(21)　　　　(22)　　　　(23)　　　　(24)

(25)　　　　(26)　　　　(27)　　　　(28)

(29)　　　　(30)　　　　(31)　　　　(32)

219

ON SUNDAYS

Mustard butter

450 g (1 lb) unsalted butter
6 g (⅛ oz) salt
100 g (3½ oz) Dijon mustard
70 g (2½ oz) crème fraîche

Place the butter in a bowl and keep in a warm spot to soften, but try not to let it melt. When it is slightly malleable transfer it into a bowl blender with the salt and mustard. Blend on high until smooth. Transfer the butter mix back into the bowl and add the crème fraîche. Use a spatula to fold them together.

Whipped soy cream

500 g (1 lb 2 oz) cultured cream
500 g (1 lb 2 oz) crème fraîche
100 g (3½ oz) white soy

Place everything into a bowl and whip to soft peaks with a whisk. Transfer to a container and chill.

Macadamia cream and shiitake oil

Macadamia cream

250 g (9 oz) macadamia nuts
60 g (2 oz) bread
1 garlic clove, peeled
100 g (3½ oz) vegetable oil
30 g (1 oz) sherry vinegar

Shiitake oil

500 g (1 lb 2 oz) shiitake mushrooms
500 g (1 lb 2 oz) portobello mushrooms
10 g (¼ oz) dried mixed mushrooms
400 g (14 oz) vegetable oil

Macadamia cream

Soak the bread in cold water for 4 minutes, then gently squeeze out any excess. Put everything, except the oil and vinegar, in an upright blender with 350 g (12½ oz) water and blend on high until smooth-ish. Slowly pour in the oil and blend until smooth. Season with salt and the sherry vinegar.

Shiitake oil

Preheat your wood-fire oven and light a fire. Using a sharp knife, cut the mushrooms down into rough 5 mm (¼ in) dice. Working in batches, cook them in the vegetable oil in a cast-iron pan in the wood oven until soft. Once you have cooked them all, place the mushrooms in a large tamis sieve over high heat over the fire so that they smoke and dry to a chewy consistency, around 3–4 hours. Once semi-dried put them into an upright blender with the dried mushrooms, oil and a good pinch of salt. Blend this on high speed until the oil heats up to around 70°C (158°F). Pour into a clean container and leave to cool.

To finish

Scoop some of the macadamia cream into a small serving dish. Give the shiitake oil a good stir then spoon a little alongside the cream. At the restaurant we channel a ying and yang vibe for this.

ON SUNDAYS

Fish skin stock

Makes 1 kg (2 lb 3 oz)

1 kg (2 lb 3 oz) skins from white fish

This may be controversial, but I prefer stocks to taste of what they're made of rather than be weird fish-leek-vegetable broths like we have always been taught to make in kitchens. The beautiful thing with only using the skins here is that the stock they produce is fishy but incredibly clean-tasting, and the gelatine that comes out of the skins gives the stock that lip-sticking quality you chase in a good protein stock. Place the skins in a pot and cover with cold water. Slowly bring up to the boil and simmer for 45 minutes, regularly skimming any foam that rises to the surface. When finished, carefully ladle off the liquid and strain through a fine-mesh sieve.

Beef stock

Makes 5 kg (11 lb)

10 kg (22 lb 11 oz) beef shin bones

A beef stock should taste of beef. Obvious? You would be surprised … If you want additional flavourings, they can be added at a later point. You could make half the quantity of the recipe, if you like, but it's an annoyingly long job so you might as well make enough of it and have plenty to store. Roast the bones at 200°C (390°F) until deeply golden brown, then transfer to a large stockpot. Cover with cold water and bring up to the boil then reduce the heat right down and simmer for 8–10 hours, skimming regularly. Strain off the stock through a fine-mesh sieve.

Shio koji

Makes approx. 400 ml (13½ fl oz)

250 g (9 oz) koji
120 g (4½ oz) salt

Mix the koji and salt in a glass jar with 540 g (1 lb 3 oz) water and keep at room temperature for a minimum of 3 weeks. We make flavoured shios by substituting a portion of the water for another liquid (e.g. lemon juice), or by adding a spice or aromatic. When the liquid is incredibly savoury and the koji slurry has settled to the bottom, carefully ladle the shio liquid off the top.

Lemon dressing

Makes 570 g (1 lb 4 oz)

120 g (4½ oz) lemon juice
35 g (1¼ oz) chardonnay vinegar
8 g (¼ oz) sugar
8 g (¼ oz) salt
400 g (14 oz) olive oil

Place all the ingredients in a tall jug with 40 g (1½ oz) water and blend with a hand-held blender until emulsified.

Fermented juices and vegetables

Makes 1 kg (2 lb 3 oz)

1 kg (2 lb 3oz) vegetables or juice
50 g (1¾ oz) whey from naturally fermented yoghurt or a past ferment
25 g (1 oz) salt

Place everything in a large vacuum-pack bag, shake well and then seal on high pressure. The ferment will take a minimum of 3 weeks to reach the required sourness. During this time it will begin to create gas and the bag will blow up like a balloon, so make sure you release this and re-vac it or it will explode and make a bloody mess. Ferments can then be kept in the fridge to halt their activity.

Fermented honey

Makes 1 kg (2 lb 3 oz)

1 kg (2 lb 3 oz) honey
50 g (1¾ oz) whey from naturally fermented yoghurt

Place the honey and whey in a sterilised glass jar with 200 g (7 oz) water and mix thoroughly. Cover with a tight-fitting lid and leave to ferment for around 6 months. Stir the ferment every week to help speed it along.

Try adding different aromats, flowers or herbs to this base.

Infused vinegars

Makes 1 kg (2 lb 3 oz)

100 g (3½ oz) leaves, herbs or flowers of your choice
1 kg (2 lb 3 oz) white vinegar

Place the aromats in a sterilised glass jar. Pour the vinegar into a small pot and warm to 65°C (149°F). Pour into the jar and seal with a tight-fitting lid. Leave to cool.

Aioli

Makes 415 g (14½ oz)

2 egg yolks
30 g (1 oz) Dijon mustard
30 g (1 oz) lemon juice
10 g (¼ oz) champagne vinegar
1 garlic clove, minced
250 g (9 oz) vegetable oil
75 g (2¾ oz) olive oil

Place everything except the oils into a bowl. Use a whisk to beat the mix until smooth, then slowly pour in the oils in a very slow, continuous stream. Whisk until thick and emulsified, then season with salt.

Index

ON SUNDAYS

ON SUNDAYS

Acknowledgements

From Royce

Thanks to Dave for your kindness and trust in letting me into your incredible brain, to Tash for making the introduction, to Roxy and Michael at Hardie Grant, and to Kalu.

From Dave

This book owes its existence to many wonderful people that have helped along the way. To Natasha, my rock and my inspiration. To my parents, Kay and Hank, for putting up with me being a shit of a teenager. To Christian for having the vision. To Jasper Avent for being my righthand man, and Harvey Noy for just being a weapon. To THEBRICKCHEF for always being the right person for the job. To all of the excellent people who have worked with us over the years. To anyone I've ever worked for for teaching me. To the team at Hardie Grant, especially Michael Harry, Ruby Goss and Roxy Ryan. To Kris Paulsen and Lee Blaylock for being incredible at what you do. Lastly, to Royce, what a pleasure it's been creating this with you, mate.

Published in 2024 by Hardie Grant Books, an imprint of Hardie Grant Publishing

Hardie Grant Books (Melbourne)
Wurundjeri Country
Building 1, 658 Church Street
Richmond, Victoria 3121

Hardie Grant Books (London)
5th & 6th Floors
52–54 Southwark Street
London SE1 1UN

hardiegrant.com/books

Hardie Grant acknowledges the Traditional Owners of the Country on which we work,
the Wurundjeri People of the Kulin Nation and the Gadigal People of the Eora Nation,
and recognises their continuing connection to the land, waters and culture. We pay our
respects to their Elders past and present.

 A catalogue record for this
book is available from the
National Library of Australia
NATIONAL
LIBRARY
OF AUSTRALIA

On Sundays
ISBN 978 1 74379 909 3

10 9 8 7 6 5 4 3 2 1

Publisher: Michael Harry, Simon Davis
Project Editor: Ruby Goss, Elena Callcott
Editor and Indexer: Andrea O'Connor
Design Manager: Kristin Thomas
Designer: Murray Batten
Photographer: Kristoffer Paulsen
Stylist: Lee Blaylock
Head of Production: Todd Rechner
Production Controller: Jessica Harvie

Colour reproduction by Splitting Image Colour Studio
Printed in China by Leo Paper Products LTD.

 The paper this book is printed on is from FSC®-certified forests and other
sources. FSC® promotes environmentally responsible, socially beneficial
and economically viable management of the world's forests.